Dancing with Angels

The Cancer Chronicles:
A Journey of Faith

Dancing
with Angels

The Cancer Chronicles:
A Journey of Faith

Glenn Lussky

with contributions by Becky Lussky

Skrive Publications
Miramar Beach, Florida
U.S.A.

Copy Editor: Dan Madson
Cover Design: Liz Nitardy
Cover photos were provided by Sarah Peterson, founder of the non-profit
p.s., I love you, inc.

Printed in the U.S.A.

ISBN 978-1-952037-01-6

Skrive Publications
Miramar Beach, Florida
(608) 332-6986

www.skrivepublications.com

Dedication

In loving memory of Becky Lussky,
who inspired many with her love for Jesus

Contents

Acknowledgements

I would like to thank all the people who followed our cancer journey in real time and supported Becky and me with thoughts, prayers, and spiritual support. As noted many times in this book, that support meant a great deal to both of us!

Thanks also to those who suggested that Becky's posts on social media would make great daily devotionals – or even a great book. I hope my effort to assemble her writings, along with my insights and background information, comes close to meeting the expectations of what such a book should look like. The blessings we received from each of you and from our Lord were countless.

Thank you to Becky's brother and sister, Dan Madson and Liz Nitardy, who wrote the Foreword. They both provided great insights into Becky's life, a life which was always characterized by her love for Jesus and the deep faith she had in Him until the end of her earthly life.

Thank you to Skrive Publications for being a great partner in sharing my interest in writing and publishing this book. Their input and efforts to strengthen the manuscript and get the book ready for publication helped me turn an idea into a reality.

Finally, **Thanks be to God, who gives us the victory through our Lord Jesus Christ (1 Corinthians 15:57).** Thank you, Lord, for the comfort you provided through your Word to Becky, me, our family, and all those who loved Becky. What a blessing to have that comfort and strength, both during and after this journey!

-Glenn Lussky

Foreword

Becky was many things to me. She was the consummate big sister. She relished tending to the typical things that fall to the oldest sibling like organizing events for family members' special occasions and hosting holiday celebrations. Her home was always open and she made me feel as if she had waited all week to see me when I entered. She was my confidant. It didn't matter what challenges I faced, I would always call her first. Her ability to listen to me and others was remarkable.

She was a Christian example of a godly wife. I watched her closely and tried to emulate the respect and kindness she showed her husband. She was a loving mother to my nephew and nieces. Her love was often demonstrated by the hours she spent holed up in her sewing room creating costumes, prom or matching Easter dresses. She was my friend. Family gatherings routinely saw us rising early for walks before everyone else was up. No subject left untouched. She was my kindred spirit. We agreed on important and unimportant matters and found ourselves spending our energy and time on similar endeavors. She was a connected godmother to our four sons, always remembering to send them letters on the occasion of their baptisms. And she was my Solomon. Of anyone I have known, she was best able to listen to a scenario or a problem and quickly discard everything that didn't matter. She would calmly and quietly sum up what was important and leave me with a nugget: "Don't overthink this one." "Stand in her shoes." "As a mom, do what's right, not what your kids want." "Let them fail." "Do what you do well. Let others do the other stuff." "Always remember, you live under grace."

That's quite a list. However, none of the above tributes matter as much as what Becky did best for me. She was my pointer. Without fail, throughout our 52 years spent together on this earth, and especially in her last year of life, she pointed me to Jesus.

Becky didn't view cancer as a negative thing in her life. She never fought cancer. She may be the only person I'll ever know who developed a harmonious relationship with the disease, realizing early on that God was using it to remind her of her most important job on earth – to point others to Jesus. In her words, her greatest cancer, sin, had already been cured. Because of Christ's power over her spiritual cancer, earthly cancer had no power over her.

In one of our last conversations, she reminded me that she was human. She confided that she was envious of me. I was going to be able to enjoy my grandchildren. She wouldn't be given that opportunity. In turn, I confided in her that I was envious. She was going home to Jesus' arms, the place I often long to be. She smiled when I said that, and then nodded her head, her eyes closed, her jaw set.

Everyone who has gathered in her kitchen or sat in her classroom over the years has read the first two lines of her favorite hymn verse on quilted banners: "Thanks to Thee, O Christ victorious; Thanks to Thee, O Lord of Life." The banners will most likely remain, doing just what she had planned on them doing – pointing. We sang this hymn verse quietly and resolutely together on a phone call one evening. It had become crystal clear in her mind that she would use every moment of her cancer journey to point others to Jesus. It will remain my fondest memory.

"Thanks to Thee, O Christ victorious! Thanks to Thee, O Lord of life!
Death hath now no power o'er us, Thou hast conquered in the strife.
Thanks because Thou didst arise And hast opened Paradise!
None can fully sing the glory Of the resurrection story."

-Liz Nitardy, Becky's sister

Becky was the oldest of five Madson siblings – the junior matriarch of the family. My oldest memories of Becky are from Trail, MN, the place we were born. Our father was the pastor of five small rural congregations from 1959 - 1964. Becky made friends with some kids who lived next door, all girls. Since I had nobody to play with, I tagged along with them until they grew tired of me bothering them, at which point they would yell, "Get away from us, pesty-fly!"

We moved to Luverne, MN, in the mid-60s, where we lived in a neighborhood populated predominantly by boys. As a grade schooler, Becky was a good athlete and could hold her own in all the neighborhood games we played from softball to basketball to kick the can. She suffered a serious injury one summer while playing softball during Vacation Bible School. She took a line drive right in the eye and ended up in the hospital for a week. We all wondered if she'd see again!

From the time she was a little girl, Becky was smart, studious and attentive, no matter what she was doing. She always got straight A's in school. She always practiced her music lessons on time, be it piano, clarinet or violin. To her credit, she also helped keep her two younger brothers from getting in too much trouble.

We moved to Wisconsin in 1971 and attended a small country school near

Madison. It was an idyllic place to spend our junior high years before we headed off to Lakeside Lutheran High School in nearby Lake Mills. In high school, Becky was involved in music and drama, eventually becoming the leader of the marching band. She also tried her hand at sports at a time when girls were starting to participate more in basketball, softball and track. Since my brother and I also played sports, our father spent most of his leisure time driving to games and watching us play. To Becky's consternation, many years after graduating, dad asked her, "Did you play basketball in high school?" (She did). Becky worked hard at her schoolwork, studying to the wee hours on most school nights. My brother and I, on the other hand, dropped our books on the dining room table when we got home and picked them up again in the morning. My high school friends and I gave her more grief than she deserved, but we all got along.

Becky and I both became teachers. I taught middle school at Holy Cross Lutheran in Madison, WI. She taught Spanish at Luther High School in Onalaska, WI.

I'll never forget the night Becky told us she had cancer at our family Christmas dinner in Madison. She was calm and forthright about it. At the time, we had no idea she was about to embark on a long, painful journey. Breast cancer was followed by multiple bouts with ovarian cancer. Throughout the years Becky struggled with these diseases, she never once complained. At least not to me. She was a paragon of faith. Her goal from the outset, as she always said, was to bring glory to God. In that regard, Becky was a champion. She posted long, personal messages on social media; she encouraged others who were struggling with similar illnesses; she talked about her faith in Jesus to her healthcare workers. Throughout her life, but especially during her struggles with cancer, Becky let her light shine. The impact she had on countless people may not be known until we get to heaven, but it was significant.

We all miss Becky's love for life, her sense of humor and her diligent modeling of daughter, sister, wife, mother, grandmother, teacher and friend. May God rest her soul.

-Dan Madson, Becky's brother

Preface

When my wife Becky was living with cancer, she was very public regarding the entire process. As you will read in this book, she shared many of the emotions related to her cancer journey in her Facebook posts. This was her way of keeping people informed regarding her health status. But it was much more than that.

Becky's understanding and application of God's Word during her cancer journey was evident in her posts. I don't know how many times people expressed to me how much they loved reading what she wrote or how they anxiously awaited to see what she would post next. They all seemed to appreciate how Becky's posts strengthened their faith. I believed they also appreciated seeing how God's Word brought her peace during this challenging time in her life.

This book is built around Becky's regular Facebook posts, along with a number of other personal unpublished letters and writings. Interspersed with her writings are my comments and memories – the story behind the story, so to speak. But it's Becky's words that form the foundation of the book. They were the inspiration and reason that made the story possible.

While this book is written chronologically – somewhat in the form of a memoir – it is also a commentary on living with cancer and dying from cancer. It reflects the real challenges and emotions we have as human beings when dealing with terminal health issues. It also underscores the power of God's Word during these difficult times. The overarching message of this book is that faith matters to believers when faced with suffering on this earth.

Our faith in Jesus as our Savior made a huge difference to Becky and me as we navigated the many challenges and emotions related to her illness. We were routinely buoyed up by our Christian friends who journeyed with us and supported us with prayers and passages from God's Word.

To the Christian, the blessings we talk about in this book will likely be reassuring and strengthening, not only in dealing with challenges like cancer, but also in your approach to daily living. To those who aren't sure about your relationship with God, I hope this book helps you see how God's promises to all of us can make a difference in how you live your lives, trusting in Him for all you need, both now and in eternity.

May our words and God's holy Word be a blessing to you as we take you through the Cancer Chronicles, a Journey of Faith!

Introduction

My wife was the most important person in my life. She was also an incredible mother and grandmother who was dearly loved by her children and grandchildren. Her cancer diagnosis in 2014 had a profound impact on our family. We experienced grief and sadness right from the start. However, those emotions were always colored with hope and joy. We began a journey of unknown length and difficulty – one we knew would change our family forever.

My wife's name was Rebecca. I thought it was beautiful name. Her parents always called her Rebecca, but I got to know her as Becky. Some of her uncles and cousins called her Guppa; her children called her Mom; her grandchildren called her Grandma; her Spanish students called her Señora. I loved her by all those names, but she was always Becky to me.

From the time Becky was diagnosed with terminal cancer, we decided to be open and honest about the fear, anxiety and sorrow we would undoubtedly experience. We shared numerous stories with our friends through social media. We found that by doing so, our network of friends grew exponentially. Ultimately, many of those friends would join us on a very personal and intimate journey.

Shortly after her initial diagnosis, Becky told me that no matter what happened, one of her goals was that God would be glorified. Throughout her cancer journey, Becky leaned on God's promises for strength and always trusted His will for her life. God, on his part, continually lifted us up through his Word.

It is my hope that by recounting our journey in this book, we will continue to encourage others. Even in the most challenging circumstances, God has ordained a perfect plan for each of us.

Becky and I met in Madison, Wisconsin, in the spring of 1980. I was a senior at the University of Wisconsin in Madison working on my undergraduate degree in meteorology. At the time, Becky was a sophomore at Bethany Lutheran College in Mankato, Minnesota, and was touring with the choir. A friend of mine and I attended the choir concert at Holy Cross Lutheran Church in Madison at the beginning of their spring tour.

As Becky later recalled, she and one of her friends were feeling flirty after the concert and decided to introduce themselves to us. Perhaps she was emboldened by the fact she already knew my friend from her grade school years in Luverne, Minnesota.

My recollections of that first encounter remain vague. However, the choir circled back through the area a week later and my friend and I went to a second concert. They performed at Western Koshkonong Lutheran Church, a small country parish outside Madison. Becky's father was the pastor there at the time. After the concert, my friend and I were invited to the parsonage with some of the choir members to sing some more. For the most part, we sang hymns, with Becky's mother at the piano. It turned out to be a great evening of singing with a group of talented musicians. That's when I really started noticing Becky. Not only was she attractive, but she also exuded style and class. I was more than impressed and wanted to get to know her better. However, I was informed she was dating someone else, so I figured that wouldn't work and, with some regret, moved on. At least for a few months.

I knew Becky's boyfriend. He was a high school classmate and friend of one of my sisters. During the summer of 1980 he started dating my sister, so I figured Becky must no longer be going out with him. Back in those days, before smart phones and social media, there was no simple way of finding out details of someone's relationship status. Even harder was getting to know somebody who lived in another state. You could write letters or make phone calls. I decided to call Becky. I don't recall the conversation exactly, but it went something like this:

> *Me: Would you like to get together sometime?*
> *Becky: You mean, like on a date?*
> *Me: Sure.*
> *Becky: I can't. I'm still dating Joel.*
> *Me: Really? I figured you broke up given the fact that he's been dating my sister.*
> *Becky: He is? I didn't know that. I guess I'll have to have a talk with him about that.*

The results of that conversation didn't go as I had hoped. As it turned out, Becky gave her boyfriend an ultimatum, and he stopped seeing my sister. My hopes didn't pan out and there was nothing to do but move on. Again.

I stayed in Madison for graduate school and loved it there. I had good friends with similar interests, including softball, golf, cross country skiing, and playing guitar. And meteorology, of course. I spent some time with a number of young ladies during the next couple of years while I worked on my master's degree. I was hoping to connect with someone where *everything* clicked. But it never quite did. I'm convinced things didn't work out with any of them because God had different plans for my life.

In early October, 1982, I returned to the Bethany campus to attend the weekend Homecoming festivities. As I was leaving the facility after the Homecoming banquet that evening, I ran into Becky. We said hello and chatted briefly, but that was all. It wasn't until I was driving back to Madison the next day that I learned Becky and her long-time boyfriend had broken up.

That news quickly rekindled my interest in Becky. I wrote her a letter the next day and asked if she might be interested in getting together. Sometime later, Becky told me that, after she read my letter, she had written two or three letters in return. She crumpled up each of them and threw them away because she thought her words made it sound like she was too excited. She eventually sent me a generic, newsy two-page letter which ended something like this:

> *I plan to be in Madison to visit my brother and sister-in-law over the weekend of November 5-7. Maybe we can get together sometime while I'm there. Let me know if that might work.*
>
> *Becky*

My UW friends and I had season tickets to Badger football games in those days. The team wasn't all that good back then and it was easy to get extra tickets if you needed them. Since I knew I could get an extra ticket, I sent Becky another letter asking if she might want to go to the football game on November 6th. She responded, "Yes!" Our first date was on the books. I was definitely looking forward to it!

When the day arrived, I picked her up at her brother's apartment. We arrived at the stadium and found a place to park. It rained lightly on occasion during the game that day, and Becky never cared for how the rain messed with her hair. Nevertheless, I thought she looked great!

Becky's brother, Dan, and his wife, Lisa, had told us we could come over and use their place that evening for dinner, as they had another engagement and wouldn't be home. I must have told Becky during our conversation at the game that I enjoyed playing the guitar. After the game, we stopped by my apartment to pick up my guitar and some music and headed over to their apartment. We had fun making spaghetti and, after we cleaned up, she said she wanted to hear some music.

We sat down and I started playing and singing. I was a big Dan Fogelberg fan and knew a lot of his music, so I crooned Fogelberg to her. I wasn't a great guitar player or singer, and Becky wasn't very familiar with his music, but she seemed to like it.

Prior to the date, Becky had promised herself that if it didn't go well, she would make sure she paid me for the ticket to the game. She didn't want to feel as if she owed me anything if she didn't like me. She never offered to pay for the ticket which, if I had known the promise she made to herself at that time, I would have regarded as a very good sign. When we left her brother's apartment, she followed me out to my car and gave me a good-night kiss. That was definitely a good sign. I'm pretty sure I kissed her back.

That was the beginning. We both were interested in pursuing this new relationship, so we kept in touch through the magic of the U.S. Postal Service and a few long-distance phone calls. Becky graduated from the University of Wisconsin-Eau Claire with a teaching degree and a minor in Spanish in December of 1982 and moved to Madison to find work, a challenging task back then. After 27 days of applying at nearly 60 businesses, she was hired at Vera's Bridal Shop because she was an excellent seamstress. Within a month, she also took a part-time position with the State of Wisconsin Department of Public Instruction.

She was working 60 hours a week, and I was busy with school. Still, we saw each other as often as we could. We became engaged at the end of May, 1983, and were married September 24, 1983. Clearly, God's plan for our life together was taking shape.

**Proverbs 19:21: Many are the plans in the mind of a man,
but it is the purpose of the Lord that will stand.**

*C*hapter 1
The Initial Cancer Diagnosis

I think every couple that lives in a loving marriage hopes and believes they will live out their marriage vows to a ripe old age – 'til death parts them. That's how we envisioned our life as a couple. We figured we'd grow old together with our children, grandchildren and great-grandchildren. That was our plan anyway. Obviously, God had other plans for Becky's life, for my life and for our life together.

In late November, 2008, at the age of 49, Becky had a routine mammogram. Usually, she would receive a letter in the mail telling her the mammogram results were normal. This time, however, there was a message on our answering machine asking Becky to call the Breast Care Center. She said to me, "This doesn't sound good." When she called, they wanted her to come in again to get some additional imaging done, so she went for a second mammogram and an ultrasound. They continued to see a suspicious area, so Becky was scheduled for a biopsy on December 23, 2008. They said it was probably nothing with only a 15-20% chance of testing positive for cancer, but they wanted to be sure.

I still remember that day like it was yesterday. It was December 26, 2008. We were at the Madson family Christmas gathering at Dan and Lisa's home in Madison. All the brothers and sisters and in-laws were there, along with many of their children. Becky's cell phone rang as we were about to sit down for the family Christmas dinner. It was her doctor. She took the call in a side room and when she came back, she asked me to join her out there. She told me it was the doctor calling. The biopsy results were positive. We were both quiet for a minute. Becky had breast cancer.

I don't remember much else from that time, except Becky quietly telling me she had cancer. We both had an incredulous feeling this was something that was *not* supposed to happen. Even after two mammograms, an ultrasound and the biopsy, we did not expect a cancer diagnosis. Becky didn't come from a family with a history of breast cancer. We shared a quick hug and decided this was something we should tell the family right away, since they were all there. Becky calmly walked back into the dining room and said to her family, "That was my doctor on the phone. I have cancer." I remember her father saying a special prayer for Becky at the table, asking for God's blessings on her treatment.

And He did bless her. The cancer was caught very early. DCIS (ductal carcinoma in situ), they said, which was about as early as it could be found. Pre-stage 1. Becky was told that, with treatment, she had a 98% chance of a full recovery and a complete cure of the cancer. She had a routine lumpectomy on January 22, 2009, followed by 30 radiation treatments over the course of the next six weeks. She recovered well and had regular follow-up exams with her cancer doctor. They never detected any new cancer in her breasts.

Becky was the kind of person who loved to learn. When there were new things to which she was exposed in her life, she wanted to know more about them. In relation to her breast cancer experience, she did a lot of online research and bought books which helped her better understand what she was experiencing and how it compared to what other women had experienced during various stages of breast cancer. Her experience and growing knowledge about breast cancer led her to want to share that information with other women. She put together a presentation that covered a broad range of technical information, along with her history and perspectives relating to her personal experiences. She presented this information to a number of women's groups.

In her presentation, she noted the following insights:

1. No matter what happens, God is in control. We live in an age where God has enabled medical science to better understand how to detect, diagnose and treat breast cancer.

2. If breast cancer is detected early enough, many women can still lead completely normal lives with proper treatment.

3. When you or a loved one is diagnosed with cancer, you will likely feel many emotions including fear, anger and shock. Cling to God's promises: **Deuteronomy 31:6b, 8b: The Lord your God goes with you. He will never leave you nor forsake you. Do not be afraid; do not be discouraged.**

4. There are many blessings that come from cancer. Before Becky was diagnosed with cancer, she was having somewhat of a mid-life crisis. She felt like she was getting burned out with teaching. Our youngest son went to college and we were empty nesters for the first time. She wondered what she really wanted to do with the rest of her life. She prayed this specific prayer: "God, I don't know if I can or should do this anymore (meaning teaching). I am so exhausted. I'd like a new experience. Is there a door you can open for me?" As it turned out, one of God's answers was cancer. Among the blessings she cited were these:

    a. The cancer diagnosis forced her to slow down and re-energized her.

    b. The cancer diagnosis indirectly led to the resolution of Becky's fatigue which she had been dealing with for some time. During the course of her treatments, a blood test identified a serious iron deficiency, the cause of her low energy level. Once that issue was resolved, she felt much better.

    c. The outpouring of encouragement and affirmation from students and parents gave her a renewed zeal to continue her career in the classroom.

    d. She was reinvigorated from a learning perspective. In what Becky felt was an odd kind of blessing, the cancer experience fascinated her. It gave her something new to study as well as a new avenue whereby she could help others.

5. God's Word is a great source of comfort and strength. During her experience, she noted how many well-known Bible passages became more personal to her. Though she knew and trusted Scripture her whole life, it became much more relevant and personal. She had used God's Word to comfort others in the past, but now others were doing the same for her. The complacency many Christians often feel regarding God's Word was gone. God used her initial cancer experience to intensify her focus on His promises.

6. If you are a family member, friend or acquaintance of someone diagnosed with cancer, there are many ways to help them: pray for them, and tell them you are praying for them; send them encouraging cards or notes; visit them; offer to help them with child care, meal preparation or transportation. Finally, let them know what they have meant to you.

Many of these revelations from her breast cancer days would eventually be magnified through the coming years when she would be faced with a more ominous diagnosis of ovarian cancer. Nevertheless, after five years of checkups following her breast cancer treatments, she was officially declared cured from her cancer in July of 2014.

Chapter 2

A New Cancer Challenge

One night in 2012, after our son Ryan moved out of the house for good, Becky and I were sitting at the kitchen island having dinner. She made a comment to me that we were now living our bonus years. At that time, the comment seemed strange to me. In my mind, our bonus years would be the years together when we had lived past our normal life expectancies. She explained what she meant. To her, bonus years would include any years beyond those where we had been overwhelmed with the day-to-day grind of working and raising a family. She felt we had entered those bonus years now that it was just the two of us enjoying life as a couple again. I told her I could live with that definition. If these were bonus years, then that's what we had!

We reveled in the feeling of being empty nesters and took full advantage of one-on-one time with each other.

Becky started to experience physical changes and nuanced symptoms in 2013 that neither she nor her doctors could quite figure out. In July, 2013, she told her primary physician of changes in pressure on her bladder, especially at night. She was 54 years old at the time and post-menopausal, so they figured this could be related to that life change. They suggested possible medications, but Becky decided to live with it rather than take drugs.

Even after that first bout with breast cancer, we had no idea that something more serious was ahead. Early in 2014, Becky and I were mapping out a six-year plan for retirement in 2020. We still had plans to grow old together.

In the spring of 2014, she noticed extra abdominal bloating and the fact that food wasn't settling as well as usual. She felt full more quickly with frequent pressure in her stomach. She also noticed tenderness in her front right hip area when she leaned against the kitchen counter. One night in June she said to me, "Something is just a little off." Nevertheless, just a month later, on July 23, 2014, at her five-year final visit with her breast cancer doctor, she was declared cancer free.

Three days later, Becky bumped her right hip area against the kitchen counter. This time it wasn't just sore – it was painful. She felt that location and noticed a lump, where there wasn't one on the left side. She thought to herself, "I should get this checked out", so she scheduled an appointment with her primary physician on July 28, 2014. At the checkup, the doctor brought in a surgeon colleague to assess the lump with her. It was a lymph node that was quite tender and larger than normal. The surgeon suggested a biopsy, which they performed on Friday, August 1, 2014.

Becky was told they would have biopsy results by the following Tuesday or Wednesday. She went to bed a bit anxious Monday night and woke up in the middle of the night with these words running through her head, **God is our refuge and strength, an ever-present help in trouble.**

The very next day, at the Onalaska Luther High School teacher's in-service meeting, Becky's principal opened with a devotion based on **Psalm 46:1: God is our refuge and strength, an ever-present help in trouble,** the very same words that had been running through her mind the night before. Becky didn't know this verse would be the basis for the devotion that day, and the principal didn't know Becky woke up with those words running through her head. Both Becky and I believed it was God's unique way of calming her even before she received the new cancer diagnosis that was to come just days later.

By late afternoon, Wednesday, August 6, 2014, Becky had not received any results from her doctor, so she called the doctor's nurse. They said the results were still pending. We went forward with plans to go up north and spend a little time there with friends. On Friday, August 8, we were beginning our drive home in the late morning when our daughter, Karyn, called us. She said we were supposed to call Becky's breast cancer doctor right away. Becky called him, and the doctor was noticeably shaken when he said, "I can't believe I'm telling you this. The biopsy tested positive for cancer." Just 16 days after closing the door on breast cancer and declaring she was cancer free, he was now telling her that, once again, she had cancer. He rescheduled his afternoon so he could meet with us at 4:00 p.m. when we returned to town. We knew it wasn't encouraging news that he wanted to meet with us as soon as possible.

To say our four-hour ride home was difficult would be an understatement. We shared a lot of emotions. Looking back, this was the start of our grieving process. We didn't know for sure what type of cancer it was but suspected it would be bad news. We knew enough about cancer to know that a lymph node biopsy that showed cancer meant the cancer was not contained and would likely be advanced in nature. Even so, we had no idea what we were dealing with.

When we met with the doctor late that afternoon, he noted that while the cancer was in her lymph node, the lymph system wasn't the primary source. Most likely that's why the results took so long. The doctors probably knew they were dealing with cancer earlier in the week, but they wanted to learn more about the source before they spoke with us. We scheduled a PET scan for Tuesday, August 12, 2014. Then we called our children to tell them what we knew.

Over the weekend, Becky and I each did our own online research. There were a number of cancers we thought were possibilities, but we both came to the same conclusion. Based on all of her earlier symptoms, we both suspected this was most likely ovarian cancer that had already begun to spread. If that was the case, we knew our lives were about to change dramatically. We knew a little bit about stage 4 ovarian cancer, as two family friends had recently dealt with the same cancer. Both failed rapidly within nine months of their diagnoses. Our online research indicated the mean life expectancy for a stage

4 ovarian cancer diagnosis was approximately 21 months. If this is what Becky had, we realized her life expectancy could be just a year or two.

After Becky's morning PET scan on August 12, 2014, we met with her breast cancer doctor. He confirmed stage 4 ovarian cancer. She had a four centimeter tumor on her right ovary, additional cancer nodules in her abdominal cavity, and cancer throughout her lymph system from neck to groin. The words Becky's doctor said to us were unforgettable. He said, "This cancer is incurable and inoperable, but it is treatable." After our meeting, we were stunned, even though we had suspected the worst. We went to Riverside Park and sat down on a bench next to the river while we digested this life-changing news. I held Becky in my arms for a long time and we grieved together. The reality and the sadness were overwhelming. We eventually called our pastor and went to see him in his office to give him the news. He opened his Bible and shared with us **Isaiah 43:1-3: Do not fear, for I have redeemed you; I have called you by name; you are mine. When you pass through the waters, I will be with you; and when you pass through the river, they will not sweep over you. When you walk through fire you will not be burned; the flames will not set you ablaze. For I am the Lord your God, the holy one of Israel, your Savior.** These words of comfort were the beginning of our understanding of how God would be with us as we began this difficult journey.

We visited a few of our close friends that day. Later, we called our children, parents and siblings to tell them. All of these visits and calls were painful. The news was difficult for us to express and came as a shock to everyone. One day, we were living normal lives; suddenly, we were faced with the prospect of the impending death of someone close and important to all of us.

Chapter 3
The Journey Begins

A friend of ours named Karl died from leukemia in May, 2013. After the funeral, we were driving home and Becky said, "If I ever get cancer again, I want to be just like Karl." Specifically, she was referring to how he handled his cancer. Throughout his illness, Karl's faith in Jesus became his strength and focus. He consistently proclaimed to others what a difference his faith and trust in Jesus made to him. Becky saw that and wanted to do the same.

Right from the start, Becky wanted to be open and honest about her cancer journey. The day before we met with our ovarian cancer doctor, Becky wanted to share her new life challenge with others. She updated her status on Facebook with the following post:

[August 13, 2014]

Dear Friends,

God has chosen to put a challenge in my life. Yesterday I learned that I have ovarian cancer. The cancer involves the right ovary. It has spread throughout the abdomen and to lymph nodes in the groin, pelvis, para-aortic region, chest, and base of my neck. Initial treatment will likely be chemotherapy, as many of the nodal sites are not accessible by surgery. Glenn and I were not surprised by the diagnosis, but it was still numbing to hear stage 4 cancer. We meet with doctors tomorrow to learn more about treatment options. I have times of anxiety but an overall sense of calm that I am in God's hands and that His plan for my life is perfect! Our pastor pointed us to **Isaiah 43:1-3. But now this is what the Lord says – he who created you, O Jacob, he who formed you, O Israel: 'Fear not, for I have redeemed you; I have summoned you by name; you are mine. When you pass through the waters, I will be with you; and when you pass through the rivers, they will not sweep over you. When you walk through the fire, you will not be burned; the flames will not set you ablaze. For I am the Lord, your God, the Holy One of Israel, your Savior.** How thankful I am that I am God's redeemed child. Please pray for me and my family. Your spiritual encouragement will lift me up! To God be the glory!

Among the comments posted from friends were these encouraging words:

- You are in our prayers, Señora! **Psalm 46:10: Be still and know that I am God! I am present in your pain, and I always will remain your comforter and friend.**
- We don't always understand God's plan but always know it is part of a bigger plan for our lives. I pray for your constant calm and strength and the peace that passes all understanding. Sending you a hug right now.
- Becky, Isaiah and God are correct. You *are* redeemed. He is always with you! And you can trust Him and praise Him every moment, no matter what. Your whole life is a testament to that belief, Becky, and now you can display God's handiwork in your life by your strength, your attitude, your role modeling through severe challenges and your unswerving faith. **1Thessalonians 15:16: Be joyful always; pray continually.** I join you in fervent prayer for God's perfect will for your life and the lives of your family.

- **Proverbs 16:9: A man's heart plans his way, but the Lord directs his steps!** He will be leading you through this, Becky! May God bless you with strength, patience, and hope as you continue on this journey!
- So sorry to hear this news. I opened my Bible and my eyes were drawn to this passage in Psalms. **The Lord is my light and my salvation; whom shall I fear? The Lord is the strength of my life; of whom shall I be afraid?** You are in my prayers!
- May you find comfort and courage in God's plethora of promises to you, his dear child. I share with you for that purpose **Isaiah 41:10: So do not fear, for I am with you. Do not dismayed for I am your God. I will strengthen you and help you. I will uphold you with my righteous right hand.**

We learned immediately how sharing our journey with others helped do so much more than just let people know what was happening in our lives. Throughout her illness, thousands of people sent Bible passages, hymn verses and encouraging notes. Neither Becky nor I could adequately explain how much all those comments meant and encouraged us along the way. We read every one of them. There was power in all the spiritual and personal encouragement sent our way. I know social media has its problems, but this was one way it was truly wonderful! Our Facebook friends became an important part of our support structure during this difficult journey.

We met with Becky's ovarian cancer doctor Thursday, August 14, 2014. He suggested six rounds of chemotherapy. When we asked about options, he indicated we basically had two: do nothing or try chemo. He indicated chemo is effective for many, but not all women, and it *could* give an initial remission of up to a number of years. If we did nothing, Becky would likely die within three to six months. That seemed like an easy decision. Together, we decided to give chemo a try.

Becky shared this with her Facebook friends:

[August 14, 2014]

Dear friends,

Today we met with my oncologist to discuss a treatment plan. I have decided to follow an 18-week course of chemotherapy which will begin sometime in the next two weeks. My doctor was honest with me and said my cancer is not going to go away, but that the chemo is designed to knock it back, hopefully for months, if not years. Each person responds differently to the chemo, but statistically speaking,

80% of women experience positive results after this first round. That's encouraging!

Now that we have a plan in place, I am ready to move forward, completely confident God knows exactly what I need. I have a renewed appreciation for the gift of time and how precious each day is. Rejoice with me that I am a child of God through the waters of baptism and that my heavenly Father is working all things for my good. Please continue to pray for my spiritual and physical strengthening. Your loving support is so much appreciated!

Jeremiah 29:10: "For I know the plans I have for you," declares the Lord, "plans to prosper you and not to harm you, plans to give you hope and a future."

Becky mentioned a renewed appreciation for the gift of time and the preciousness of each day. A terminal illness is a great reminder that life is temporary for all of us. It also helped both of us focus on trying to live each day to its fullest. It's easy to get caught up in the minutia of day-to-day living and fretting over little things. Life often gets so busy that we neglect to take time to appreciate our friends, our family and the blessings we have been given. Terminal cancer helped us put those things into perspective and focus on things that are truly important. For us, it meant refocusing on our relationship as husband and wife as well as relationships with our family, our friends and, most importantly, our Savior. We experienced a feeling of greater purpose and immediacy in our daily living. We focused on our blessings as we had never done before. Becky and I became much better at what she called purposeful living.

School started for her students the following week. At this point, Becky was ready to resign her Spanish teaching position immediately. I was less certain she would need to, as we didn't yet know how the chemo would impact her ability to teach. We invited the school principal over for a visit and he encouraged Becky to wait to see how things played out. He graciously told her the school would do whatever they needed to do to help cover for her whenever she needed recovery time. He also told her that her students would likely learn many lessons from her that year that would extend well beyond the classroom. Becky agreed to give it a try.

Becky went into her classroom on Monday, the day before her students were to arrive. On her wall under the windows, her Junior Class students had put together a signed poster with two Bible passages: **God is our refuge and**

strength, an ever-present help in trouble, and **Be still and know that I am God**. At the bottom it said, "We are praying for you, Señora Lussky."

Becky posted on her Facebook page:

[August 18, 2014]

Thank you, class of 2016, for your encouraging words! Looking forward to seeing you on Thursday! Gracias por todo. Señora

Two days later, she followed that with a post to everyone:

[August 20, 2014]

Dear friends,

Tomorrow I begin my 20th year of teaching Spanish at Luther High School. I have never been more excited to start school. Transitioning from traditional language instruction to target-language (immersion) teaching two years ago has given new life and meaning to my teaching. I love teaching Spanish, and I love connecting with the kids! What I wasn't planning on was a cancer diagnosis the week before school started. It's still surreal. What was God thinking? After all these years, I finally get it with regards to teaching, and now this? How could He let this happen? **Romans 11:33-34: Oh, the depth of the riches both of the wisdom and knowledge of God! How unsearchable are His judgments and unfathomable His ways! For who has known the mind of the Lord, or who became His counselor?**

Our school year theme is based on **Psalm 46:10: Be still and know that I am God.** God is reminding me who is in control. Thank goodness He *is* in control! How arrogant it is when we think our plans are better than His. And so, the school year begins under different circumstances than I had expected.

The Board of Control has graciously given me its blessing to teach through chemo. Sometimes I think I'm crazy to think I can do this, but if I don't try, I'll never know. I have a specific prayer request: pray that I can tolerate chemo and continue to teach this first semester.

I begin my chemo treatment on Friday, August 29. I don't know what to expect. Right now, I feel fine, so it's hard to imagine not feeling fine. My hair will fall out. My vanity rebels at the thought. Two of

13

my colleagues have suggested I make use of my stash of drama wigs. They said I should pick out a different wig each day. I am thankful they can make me laugh.

"Be still and know that I am God." God is comforting me. "Be calm," He says, "I have taken care of your sin, your most serious illness, and I will walk with you every step of the way through your cancer journey." My favorite Bible passage is from **1 Corinthians 15:57: But thanks be to God, who gives us the victory through our Lord Jesus Christ.** Christ's victory is my victory. To God be the glory!

Becky used Facebook to ask for specific prayers. We *know* many people prayed specific prayers for comfort, for patience, for encouragement and many other blessings throughout her journey. Becky's colleagues, students and former students, along with the students' parents and many friends, were incredible. We experienced an overwhelming flood of support during those initial days and weeks that never seemed to let up throughout her cancer journey. What a wonderful blessing to have so many Christian friends praying for us and sharing their love for us on a regular basis.

[August 25, 2014]

Dear Friends,

Thank you for your spiritual encouragement and prayers on my behalf! It's overwhelming to be the recipient of such kindness. I was reading chapter two of 2 Corinthians last night and verse three jumped out at me: **Praise be to the God and Father of our Lord Jesus Christ who comforts us in all our troubles, so that we can comfort those in any trouble with the comfort we ourselves have received from God.** That's exactly what's playing out in my life right now!

I feel blessed that school is going well. The students give me so much energy. I anxiously await my first chemo treatment on Friday. It will be good to know how my body is going to respond so I have a better idea what to expect these next 18 weeks. I am especially thankful for my chemo sisters, Kris, Nancy and Lisa, who have given me a realistic peek into the possible side effects I may experience. I am learning that everyone's journey is unique. Continue to rejoice with me that I am God's own dear child and He is beside me every step of the way.

I walk with Jesus all the way,
His guidance never fails me;
Within His wounds I find a stay
When Satan's power assails me:
And by His footsteps led,
My path I safely tread.
In spite of ills that threaten may,
I walk with Jesus all the way.
[Evangelical Lutheran Hymnary (ELH 252:5)]

Becky loved hymns. She loved the spiritual messages in the verses. As she started penning her posts, she would remember hymn verses that reflected the theme of her message. Her favorite hymns became the closing signature of many of her posts. This particular verse is from *I Walk in Danger All the Way,* one of her favorite hymns.

On Friday, August 29, Becky shared her thoughts three times – a quick post early in the morning, another after an early evening visit from a dear young Christian friend, and her final post later in the evening. Those posts follow:

[August 29, 2014]

Dear Friends,

This is the day the Lord has made; let us rejoice and be glad in it! Today I begin my chemo journey. I am nervous but not afraid. God is filling me with peace that only He can give. Paul writes in **Philippians 4:6-7: Do not be anxious about anything, but in every situation, by prayer and petition, with thanksgiving, present your requests to God. And the peace of God, which transcends all understanding, will guard your hearts and your minds in Christ Jesus.** Today is also the funeral service of my dear Aunt Naomi. I am sad that I will miss her victory celebration, but I rejoice with my loved ones that she is in heaven with her Savior. **Job 19:25-26: I know that my Redeemer lives, and that in the end He will stand upon the earth. And after my skin has been destroyed, yet in my flesh I will see God.** We are victorious through Christ.

[August 29, 2014]

Tonight, Obi and his family stopped over to visit. Obi brought along a card for me with a gift of $165 that he raised on my behalf at his lemonade stand last Saturday. Amazing! He also raised similar amounts of money for three other friends who are suffering with cancer! Quadruple amazing! Thank you, Obi, from the bottom of my heart for letting the love of Jesus shine in your life!

Dear Mrs. Lussky
you can use this money
to ijoy yourself.

Get
Well Soon! from obi

Obi was an eight-year-old, the son of a pastor in our Luther High School community, who had developed childhood cancer. He was nearing the end of his life at that time but wanted to do something nice for Becky. His visit with Becky was incredibly thoughtful and touching.

[August 29, 2014]

Dear Friends,

A great day! This morning I woke up before my alarm went off as I do on so many mornings. The song that kept running through my head was the Spanish song taken from **Psalm 118:24: Este es el día que hizoel Señor; me gozaré y le alabaré (This is the day that the Lord has made; let us rejoice and be glad in it).** We often start the day in Spanish class with this echo song. When Glenn walked into the bathroom 20 minutes later, his first words to me were, "This is the day the Lord has made; let us rejoice and be glad in it." Before that time, he had *never* greeted me like that in the morning in almost 31 years of marriage. I know it wasn't a coincidence that these words were on both of our hearts and minds. God put them there to set the tone for the day ahead of us. And set the tone it did for another day of grace!

I had my port placement first, minor surgery with conscious sedation. The nurse called it happy medicine. From the port placement clinic, Glenn wheeled me across the skywalk to the cancer center where I was settled into the chemo infusion room. I spent the next four-and-a-half hours in a comfortable recliner hooked up to an IV machine via my new handy-dandy port. A saline solution cleaned the port, followed by an anti-nausea medication to keep me from getting sick. Much to my happy surprise it worked! The Benadryl, meant to keep my body from having an allergic reaction to the chemo, made me tipsy and tired, but it kept allergic reactions at bay. Next came a three-hour infusion of Taxol, the first of two chemo drugs in my chemo cocktail. Glenn read his book in a chair next to mine. He also snuck out and ran some errands while I dozed in my chair. The second and final chemo drug was Carboplatin. This infusion lasted 35 minutes. And then it was over. I had survived my first round of chemotherapy.

What a relief to have the experience behind me. The medical staff was excellent! Now I know what to expect from the infusion part of the treatment. What I still don't know is the kind of side effects I will experience. So far, I haven't had any! Did I mention it's been a great day?! I know the side effects will come. To be perfectly honest, I am not looking forward to pain and discomfort associated with side effects! But getting back to the great day… I got to spend time with my honey, Glenn. Mike, Karyn and the boys stopped by on their way up to the lake so I got to see my buddies, Isaac and Matthias, and get hugs from Karyn and Mike. We had BLT's for supper with Glenn's beautiful garden tomatoes. Texts, calls and snapchats from friends and family, combined with thousands of prayers lifted up on our behalf, encouraged both of us. The visit with Obi and family was icing on the cake. It was another wonderful day of God's grace!

> All praise to Thee my God this night
> For all the blessings of the light.
> Keep me, O keep me king of kings,
> Beneath Thine own almighty wings.
> Forgive me Lord, for Thy dear Son
> The ill that I this day have done.
> That with the world, myself, and Thee
> I, ere I sleep at peace may be.
> **[Christian Worship (CW 592:1)]**

17

Chapter 4
Chemo Reality Sets In

The first two days after her initial chemo infusion, Becky felt fairly normal. We attended a wedding the following day, and Becky felt pretty good, even spending some time on the dance floor. But the poison designed to kill cancer cells wreaks havoc with other cells as well. Things got tough in the days that followed. I posted a quick update to let everybody know how she was doing.

[September 2, 2014]

A couple of tough days yesterday and today for Becky as she figures out how the chemo is impacting her system and what she needs to do to counteract those side effects. We're hoping we got a good start on that today and that she'll feel more comfortable tomorrow. One day at a time. Thanks for your continued prayers.

The following day, Becky provided her own update:

[September 3, 2014]

Dear Friends,

I have to admit that my updates are easier to write when I feel good. The last three days I have been struggling with pain issues. Some are related to chemo; others are related to the cancer. Feeling crummy has made me realize how much I have taken for granted the countless days of good health that God has blessed me with over the years! Relief from the physical pain comes from trying a variety of drugs and dosages to see what may or may not work. Relief from the spiritual pain of sin comes from the comfort of the Gospel. I find peace seated at the piano, playing and singing the beautiful hymns that overflow with the message of love that God has for me, His child. How I treasure those same hymns that are also committed to memory. The words still my soul when I hurt, when I'm afraid.

> By grace I'm saved, grace free and boundless;
> My soul, believe and doubt it not.
> Why stagger at this word of promise?
> Has Scripture ever falsehood taught?
> No; then this word must true remain;
> By grace you too will life obtain.

> By grace God's Son, our only Savior,
> Came down to earth to bear our sin.
> Was it because of your own merit
> That Jesus died your soul to win?
> No, it was grace, and grace alone,
> That brought him from his heavenly throne.

By grace to timid hearts that tremble,
In tribulation's furnace tried,
By grace, in spite of fear and trouble,
The Father's heart is open wide.
Where could I help and strength secure
If grace were not my anchor sure

By grace! On this I'll rest when dying;
In Jesus' promise I rejoice;
For though I know my heart's condition,
I also know my Savior's voice.
My heart is glad, all grief has flown,
Since I am saved by grace alone. **(CW 384: 1,2,4,5)**

Thankfully, the chemo effects diminished soon and Becky was able to go to school six days after her treatment.

[September 4, 2014]

Dear Friends,

Today God gave me the gift of a normal day. It was so good to be back at school! The pain and discomfort of the past few days was completely gone. My prayer has been that I will be able to tolerate chemo so that I can continue to teach. Today God answered that prayer with a resounding, "Yes!" I am thankful for a normal day.

Before Becky was diagnosed with ovarian cancer, our experiences with the disease revolved around friends who had endured short periods of treatment before they succumbed to the disease. Beth was one of those friends. She died the week after Becky's first treatment.

[September 6, 2014]

Dear friends,

Yesterday was my friend Beth's funeral. Beth was 48 years old. She was diagnosed with stage 4 ovarian cancer in January of 2014. I was stunned when I heard the diagnosis. I called my brother and asked, "Have you heard about Beth?" He had. He gave me her mailing address and I immediately wrote her a card and began to pray for her.

Though Beth and I weren't close friends, we shared a bond of friendship nonetheless. We initially met through my brother who was a teaching colleague of hers at Holy Cross Lutheran School in Madison. We celebrated together at the confirmation and graduation parties of my niece and nephews, all of whom had her as a teacher. Our lives continued to intersect when, in more recent years, we celebrated together at the graduation parties of *her* nieces and nephews who were *my* students at Luther! We shared a love for teaching and a love for our respective families. How were we to know that one day we would also share the sisterhood of ovarian cancer?

Beth's sister updated me on her condition when we would see each other at Luther events. She wasn't responding well to treatment. I continued to pray for her spiritual strengthening and physical healing. Honestly, I didn't really comprehend what Beth was going through.

That all changed when I was diagnosed with stage 4 ovarian cancer. By this time, Beth was in hospice care, nearing the end of her earthly life. I needed to talk to her so I called her the last Saturday in August. I was nervous, but I needn't have been. We had a wonderful conversation. We had a hard time believing that we were both members of the cancer club. What a strange turn of events. Beth encouraged me with the hope she had in Jesus and eternal life in heaven. When I asked if she had any specific prayer requests, she said, "Pray that my sisters can find soup that my stomach can tolerate." It was the simple request of a dying woman whose body was shutting down. I wasn't expecting that prayer request, but I prayed according to Beth's wishes. And I tucked away the moment for future reference, knowing full well that someday I might be in the same situation.

In the more difficult days after Becky's first chemo infusion, she had pain that she described as zingers, shooting pains in her abdomen, back and legs. We never knew if it was the cancer itself or the chemo fighting the cancer, but it was a noticeable symptom of her disease. When that and other symptoms subsided the following week, it was a huge boost to our confidence. The chemo was working!

[September 8, 2014]

Dear Friends,

Today I had a chemo follow-up appointment with my doctor. He was very encouraged by the fact that my cancer symptoms, specifically pelvic bloating and pain, have disappeared in the last five days. It's most likely a sign that the chemo is working!

But it gets even better. I asked him if he was a Christian. He said he struggles with that question every day. He said he hopes there is a God. I told him that he doesn't have to hope, because there *is* a God, almighty and powerful, and His Son Jesus is our Savior. He said he would like to talk about God when we meet for my appointments! New prayer request: that God the Holy Spirit will work through His Word in the heart of my doctor!

> Almighty God, your Word is cast
> Like seed into the ground;
> Now let the dew of heaven descend
> And righteous fruits abound.
> So when the precious seed is sown,
> Your quickening grace bestow
> That all whose souls the truth receive
> Its saving power may know. **(Adapted from CW 324:1,4)**

Becky knew the power of believing in Jesus as her Savior. Her faith colored every aspect of her life, including how she dealt with her cancer. She wanted others to know that as well. Her oncologist had an interest in a website devoted to Yahweh but didn't really know much about Jesus. Becky wanted him to know, because she knew that God gives us the victory through our Lord Jesus Christ.

That victory was a significant part of what was going on behind the scenes at Luther High School during the first couple of weeks of the school year. The level of support from everyone - colleagues, students and parents - was nothing short of amazing.

*C*hapter 5
Blessed by an Amazing Support System

Throughout her chemo treatments, Becky experienced incredible support from her students, colleagues and friends:

[September 9, 2014]

Dear Friends,

God continues to bless me with normal days. September is Ovarian Cancer Awareness Month and Friday was Wear Teal Day. To show their support, Luther students, faculty and staff were decked out in every shade of teal imaginable. I continue to be showered with

24

incredibly thoughtful cards, gifts, and Facebook messages from family and friends. I am especially touched by the spiritual encouragement I have received from my former students. When you leave Luther, I pray you will continue to grow in your faith through Word and Sacrament. The fruits of your faith are evident as you encourage me with the promises of Jesus my Savior.

Thank you to those of you who encourage Glenn in his caregiver role. This journey is a partnership and my dear husband has embraced his role as only he can. This month, Glenn and I will celebrate our 31st wedding anniversary. We chose as our wedding text **Psalm 136:1: O give thanks, unto the Lord, for He is good, for His mercy endures forever.** Because God's mercy endures forever, I face the future with a heart full of thankfulness, knowing that my sins are forgiven and I have a home waiting for me in heaven!

In support of Señora, the Luther Pro-Life Knights made nearly 600 teal tie-dyed shirts proclaiming the victory we have in Christ – Spanish on the front and English on the back. Teal is the color of

support for those with ovarian cancer, and the passage, as Becky noted in one of her earlier posts, was one of her favorites! The football team made their own teal shirts and took their teal photos with Señora. Similarly, the Lady Knights' volleyball team shirts were teal as well, and they provided their own unique way of showing love and support for Señora. **Faith ~ Hope ~ Confidence** was emblazoned on the shirts in Spanish! And finally, the faculty posed for their annual picture, with everyone decked out in teal.

[September 12, 2014]

Dear Friends,

Today was the last day of a wonderfully normal week at school. Pro-Life Knights sponsored Life Week and sold T-shirts to support me. Mary Bilitz designed the beautiful T-shirt around my favorite Bible passage, **1 Corinthians 15:57: Thanks be to God who gives us the victory through our Lord Jesus Christ.** Connie Bader and her Pro-Life Knights crew tie-dyed 580 shirts! I am thrilled that almost 600 people will be walking billboards proclaiming the victory we have through Christ! The teal football and volleyball team shirts were worn for the first time this week. They are *so* cool!

My doctor told me my hair would start to fall out toward the end of the second week. He was right! Wednesday I started pulling tufts out with my hand so I knew it was time. I told my students on Thursday, in Spanish, that I would be shaving my head that night and coming to school sporting a wig on Friday. This proved to be a good way to soften a potentially awkward situation for me and my students. Glenn wielded the clippers in our bathroom. Son Ryan suggested a Mohawk might be the way to go, so we accommodated that request and sent him a Snapchat before taking it all off. I wondered if this would be an emotional moment, but it wasn't. I have never really liked my hair so I wasn't all that sad to see it go.

The American Cancer Society gifts a wig to chemo patients. I really like mine and from the positive reaction I got today from students and faculty, I think it will be an okay thing to wear these next few months. I have also ordered some cute hats and turbans so I can mix things up a bit. I continue to thank God I am not experiencing extended chemo side effects during round one of chemo and as such, I am able to teach. Thank you for your continued prayers on my behalf! I will close with these verses:

> He who to this day has fed me
> And to many joys has led me
> Is and ever shall be mine.
> He who ever gently schools me,
> He who daily guides and rules me,
> Will remain my help divine.

> Well he knows what best to grant me;
> All the longing hopes that haunt me,
> Joy and sorrow, have their day.
> I shall doubt his wisdom never
> As God wills, so be it ever;
> I to him commit my way. **(CW 421:2,4)**

Four years later, it was amazing to see students and parents were still wearing these shirts around campus. What a blessing to have that support, and what a witness to others of the hope we have in our salvation!

As an aside, I might add that cutting Becky's hair that evening may not have been an emotional moment for her. However, it was for me. I had a hard time getting started with the clippers. I knew once we got started there was no turning back. It was a comfort to me that she had found a wig that looked really nice on her!

*C*hapter 6
Finding Blessings in Cancer

Some of you may be familiar with TED Talks. These are informative and inspirational presentations designed to share new ideas based on specific research and evidence. While looking through them one day, I came across one in particular that really resonated with me regarding the experiences Becky and I had encountered with cancer. This particular talk reflected something Becky had mentioned when she went through her breast cancer experience, and formed part of the presentation she gave to women's groups at that time.

I shared the TED talk with Becky, figuring she would relate. She did. Completely. To me, that talk was important enough that I wanted to share it with others. The following was my Facebook post:

[September 16, 2014]

> Six years ago, when Becky had breast cancer, she openly marveled at how that experience had been a blessing to her. It reinvigorated her in many ways. Now, with a diagnosis of a much more serious and life-threatening cancer, she again sees how God can still use these events as a gift.
>
> I came across the following TED Talk by Stacey Kramer and sent it to Becky, figuring she would relate to it. She responded, "WOW! She nailed it! That's *exactly* how I feel!"
>
> Per Stacey, here are the results of the gift of cancer:
> - It will bring your family together.
> - You will feel loved and appreciated like never before.
> - You'll reconnect with friends and acquaintances you haven't heard from in years.
> - Adoration and admiration will overwhelm you.
> - It will recalibrate what's most important in your life.
> - You'll meet new people.
> - Flowers will arrive.
> - People will say to you, "You look great!"
> - You'll be challenged, inspired, motivated and humbled.
> - Your life will have new meaning.
>
> While we all may not want this gift, she noted, "I wouldn't change my experience. It profoundly altered my life in unexpected ways. The next time you're faced with something that's unexpected, unwanted or uncertain, consider that *it just may be a gift.*"

I knew that was how Becky felt. All of the items listed in Stacey's talk were things we both experienced many times over. Even with the challenges that come with cancer, there are many truly wonderful things that resulted as well.

Over the years as a teacher, drama coach, counselor and National Honor Society advisor, Becky had opportunities to communicate with the local newspapers to promote Luther High School students, activities and events.

One of the people she worked with on occasion was Randy Erickson, a local journalist. Somehow, Randy heard about Becky's diagnosis and contacted her to do an article covering her health situation. Becky told him she would only do it if he included statements about her faith in the article. He said he would.

[September 19, 2014]

I am so thankful to La Crosse Tribune journalist Randy Erickson for honoring my request that my Christian beliefs be included in this article. To God be the glory!

Luther Teacher Finds Lessons in Cancer

Just before starting her 20th year of teaching Spanish at Luther High School in Onalaska, Becky Lussky was hit with a bombshell. After going into the clinic in early August to have a lump checked out, she had a biopsy, then a PET scan and a CT scan. Then a diagnosis: stage 4 ovarian cancer that had spread into her lymph nodes away from the abdominal cavity.

Lussky knew it was ovarian cancer before the doctors told her. After the biopsy showed cancer in her lymph node, she started doing research and found that she'd had typical symptoms for ovarian cancer, she said, "I had symptoms you wouldn't associate with a serious disease."

Typical symptoms include pelvic bloating, indigestion, feeling full and frequent need to urinate. Lussky, who is 55, thought her symptoms were just part of aging. "I didn't think anything of it," she said.

The cancer that invaded her body has such a strong foothold and has spread so much that there's no knocking it out. "Stage 4 isn't a good diagnosis," Lussky said. "The cancer is incurable but treatable."

The way doctors look at it, Lussky has a chronic condition that requires treatment, much like diabetics that require insulin. Chemotherapy, which attacks fast-growing cells, can stop the cancer from growing or spreading. But cancer can become resistant to the chemo after time, so doctors will have to change things up to find a new combination of drugs that will stop it again.

"The cancer will keep coming back," she said. "The cancer gets smart enough to regenerate.

Since her diagnosis, Lussky met a woman who has been getting treatments for her ovarian cancer for five years. On the other hand, a friend of Lussky's who was diagnosed with an aggressive cancer in stage 4 back in March, succumbed a couple weeks ago after five months of treatment.

Whatever happens now for Lussky, she said, is in God's hands. "It's really one day at a time. I wake up every morning and thank God for his grace."

Lussky, who lives in La Crescent, MN, with her meteorologist husband, Glenn, started her first round of chemo on August 29. She's experienced deep bone pain, fatigue and neuropathy in her feet, but she has not had the bad nausea that often goes with chemo, thanks to effective anti-nausea medication. As of last Friday, she had not lost her hair, but she knows that's coming.

She knew long before she was diagnosed with cancer that chemotherapy causes hair loss, but she has now learned why. The chemo attacks the fast-growing cells associated with cancer, but it also attacks the body's other fast-growing cells, such as hair and the lining of the stomach.

There have been many more profound lessons for Lussky since her diagnosis. "I've learned that God blesses me through trials, and I'm experiencing unbelievable blessings through this," she said. "I've learned that the support for me is overwhelming in terms of people praying for me, writing me, sending me cards and giving me the most incredibly thoughtful gifts."

Fellow Luther teacher Connie Bader, with whom Lussky has worked on many drama productions over the years, spearheaded a project to tie-dye hundreds of T-shirts teal, the symbolic color of ovarian cancer. A Bible verse adorned the T-shirts, English on one side and Spanish on the other: "Thanks be to God who gives us the victory through our Lord Jesus Christ."

The past two Fridays Luther High was a sea of teal, with students and staff showing their love and support for Lussky.

It's touching, but Lussky just wants to keep doing what she loves to do – teaching. "My prayer is that I can tolerate the chemo so I can continue to teach. Teaching is my passion and it just gives me so much energy to be in the classroom with the kids," she said. "I don't want to be defined by cancer, and I don't want to be defined by fear. I have hope for the future, here and in heaven. I'm hopeful because my life is in God's hands."

*C*hapter 7
Remission Through Chemo

Results from Becky's first chemo infusion were excellent. The CA-125 blood number, a test that can be useful in determining whether there is active ovarian cancer, went down from 513 before the first infusion to 81 before the second infusion. CA-125 values of 35 and under are considered to be generally in the normal range. Clearly, that test suggested things were moving in the right direction.

During the first week after Becky's cancer diagnosis, I had done some online research in various medical journals and found an article that indicated if the chemo was effective and cut the CA-125 values by at least a factor of three after each infusion, the cancer was classified as chemo-sensitive. If this happened for each of the infusions, the results were striking in terms of life expectancy. For all patients with a new stage 4 ovarian cancer diagnosis, mean length of survival was one year and nine months. For women whose cancer was chemo-sensitive, the initial and subsequent remissions prolonged their mean survival length to 4.9 years! That was a significant encouragement! It also put Becky into that group of patients who could *potentially* live eight to ten years or more with the cancer. While it was rare for anyone to be completely cured, we wouldn't limit what God could accomplish if it was His will. We didn't expect a cure, but five years seemed a lot better than a year or two. We had a ray of hope.

[September 22, 2014]

Dear Friends,

My second chemo infusion went well. I had blood work at 8:00 a.m. Glenn and I met with the doctor at 9:00 a.m. He said the blood tests for kidney and liver function and red and white blood cells all looked good. We also picked up with our spiritual conversation. Please pray that the Holy Spirit will work faith in his heart!

The chemo infusion started a little after 10:00 a.m. and finished up at 3:45 p.m. The Benadryl made me drowsy again, so I slept a lot during

the treatment. Karyn and the boys stopped by to visit. Glenn and the boys went down to the first floor to look at the birds and the fish. Grandpa and Isaac also made a trip to the men's room together. Isaac is getting to be a big boy!

No side effects to speak of at this point. My plan is to teach tomorrow. Please continue to thank God for blessing me so. Pray also that the chemo side effects continue to be held at bay so that I can teach! I will close with the ELS devotion for today. I am so glad that God is in control of my life! Please also pray for Obi! **Proverbs 16:9: The heart of man plans his way, but the Lord establishes his steps.**

Order my footsteps by Thy Word
And make my heart sincere;
Let sin have no dominion, Lord,
But keep my conscience clear.

Assist my soul, too apt to stray,
A stricter watch to keep;
And should I e'er forget Thy way,
Restore Thy wand'ring sheep. **(ELH 441:2-3)**

Less than four weeks after Obi surprised Becky with his gift to her, he was taken home to heaven. Once again, we were reminded that our lives on earth are temporary. It's a pass-through on our way to our eternal home. Still, it's difficult and sad for those of us left behind who have to learn to live without someone we love.

[September 23, 2014]

Thanking God for a normal day back in the classroom the day after my second chemo infusion. Praying for the comfort of Obi's family as they mourn the loss of their beloved son and brother. Rejoicing with them that Obi is no longer suffering here on earth but living in heaven with his Savior. **Psalm 103: Bless the Lord, O my soul, and all that is within me, bless his holy name! Bless the Lord, O my soul, and forget not all his benefits, who forgives all your iniquity, who heals all your diseases, who redeems your life from the pit, who crowns you with steadfast love and mercy, who satisfies you with good so that your youth is renewed like the eagle's.**

[September 27, 2014]

Dear Friends,

Today we attended eight-year-old Obadiah Christenson's funeral. I don't think there is anything more glorious than the victory celebration for one of God's children! I won't pretend to understand the grief and sadness that Obi's family is experiencing, but I rejoice for Obi.

Obi's uncle, Pastor Schultz, reminded us that Jesus, the Good Shepherd, came so that we have full lives in Him. Full lives not measured in years or wealth or prestige, but in the fact that our sins are forgiven and we have an eternal home waiting for us in heaven.

Obi is experiencing that life now and we have that life to look forward to!

We sang Obi's favorite hymns, *Children of the Heavenly Father, I am Jesus Little Lamb*, and the Christmas anthem, *Glory to God*. The congregation was like an angel chorus today as we sang: "Glory to God, the angels sing; Praises to Christ, the heav'nly king; Peace be on earth, good will to men, good will to men." Obi is singing in that chorus of angels, free from sin and suffering, wearing the crown of righteousness that is his through Christ.

What a wonderful thought! The fullness of our lives is not dependent on the number of years we live or the wealth or recognition we've received. In the end, our lives are full based solely on the fact that we are forgiven and, as believers in Jesus, we have an eternal home waiting for us in heaven. This was, obviously, meaningful for a family who lost a child, but it was also meaningful for us, knowing that Becky's years would likely be limited.

[September 29, 2014]

Dear Friends,

Today I began the second week of chemo cycle two. God blessed me with another normal day at school doing what I love to do! Last week, with chemo on Monday, I was able to teach Tuesday, Wednesday and Thursday, missing only Friday due to chemo side effects. In both cycle one and cycle two, day five of the first week has been my down day. For 36 hours afterward, I lose my energy and my legs and feet ache. The morning of day six I can tell the side effects are wearing off and my days become normal again. It's so strange. Why don't the side effects kick in until day five? Why are my legs and feet primarily affected?

Yesterday someone asked me, "What's the most difficult part of having cancer?" I thought for a moment and replied, "Not knowing what the future holds." When I was diagnosed with breast cancer five and a half years ago, it was early stage (DCIS) and my doctor assured me that I would have a complete recovery following surgery and radiation. With a stage 4 ovarian cancer diagnosis, however, the words recovery or cure have not been part of the discussion. The doctor says my cancer is treatable. That begs the question, "For how long?" And, so, I wonder what the future holds.

The thought of going through the rest of my life in some kind of treatment isn't overly appealing to me. I don't like the side effects of chemo, and I suspect they will get worse as time goes on. Yet I am aware that it's not just cancer patients who struggle with physical side effects in life. I pray for relief for my friends who have chronic conditions: debilitating back pain, fibromyalgia, rheumatoid arthritis, serious complications from car accidents or sickness, emotional struggles and addictions.

Through suffering, God refines us and brings us closer to Him. I wake up each morning and marvel that God has given me one more day of His grace. I don't ever want to lose this feeling of awe that I have, knowing I get one more day to spend with Glenn, one more day to interact with my students, one more day to do what I am supposed to do here in this life.

Thank you for your continued prayers and spiritual encouragement. God uses you to buoy me up and keep me focused on the heavenly prize that is ours through faith in our risen Savior, Jesus Christ!

> I lay my sins on Jesus,
> The spotless Lamb of God;
> He bears them all and frees us
> From the accursed load.
> I bring my guilt to Jesus
> To wash my crimson stains
> White in His blood most precious
> Till not a spot remains.
>
> I lay my wants on Jesus,
> All fullness dwells in Him;
> He healeth my diseases,
> He doth my soul redeem.
> I lay my griefs on Jesus,
> My burdens and my cares;
> He from them all releases,
> He all my sorrows shares. **(CW 372:1-2)**

This post gives a glimpse into the varying emotions that are a part of living with cancer. Becky wanted to know what was going to happen, and yet she didn't. She wanted to experience the awe of living each day with an appreciation for the unique blessings it would bring. She also wanted to appreciate the positive emotional blessings she realized on the days she felt normal. There was a big difference between her emotional perspective on days she was feeling poorly and those when she felt normal.

One of the interesting perspectives we gained after being impacted by cancer was that we became more aware of the challenges other people were facing. Before Becky's diagnosis, we lived in our nice little bubble, happy and carefree, doing what we needed to do every day. Once stage 4 cancer entered our lives, we became much more aware that many other people were dealing with significant physical or emotional challenges. It became clear to both of us that suffering wasn't reserved for a few. Our challenges were *not* unique. Not even close.

In one way or another, we all have struggles. We all need the presence of a loving God in our lives. We all need comfort and forgiveness. The words of **Malachi 3:2** come to mind: **But who may abide the day of his coming? And who shall stand when he appeareth? For he is like a refiner's fire.** A refiner's fire purifies. It doesn't indiscriminately incinerate everything in its path. What a blessing that God refines us through our challenges and leads us to trust in His perfect plan for our lives.

Our nephew, Kyle, married the lovely Leanna on October 4, 2014. This picture, taken at the wedding, was one of our favorites. Becky was feeling good. The chemo was knocking back her cancer, and we were there reveling in a joyous occasion. We had much to celebrate. Additionally, all the blessings of cancer, including a renewed appreciation for our lives together and the thankfulness for each day, brought us great joy. The intensity of love, joy and companionship was amplified, and that feeling is reflected in the camera lens.

Nevertheless, there was still a feeling of unease. We didn't know what Becky's future held, or how long her life would be. Our son Ryan probably felt that the most.

Our two daughters, Kristin and Karyn, married right out of college and, at the time of Kyle and Leanna's wedding, had three and two kids respectively.

Ryan was 24 and had not yet been blessed with a wife. One of his concerns was that his mother might not be around if and when he got married. Even before Kyle and Leanna's wedding, it hit him hard that he might never have a mother-son dance at his wedding

One special moment at the wedding stands out in my mind. After Kyle and Leanna had their first dance and others were invited on the floor, Ryan and Becky had their mother-son dance. It was a wonderful moment. This picture doesn't reflect it, but there were people videotaping their dance, knowing it was possible that such a dance might not take place in the future. People at the wedding who didn't know about Becky's illness were wondering why Ryan and Becky were getting so much attention during their dance. When they were told, they quickly understood and shared in the moment as well.

Clearly, one of the blessings of our cancer journey was the opportunity to reconnect with old friends. If you're like most people, you probably have friends with whom you communicate once a year, perhaps at Christmastime.

We had many such friends. Over the years, before we settled in La Crescent, MN, we had lived in Madison, WI, Salt Lake City, UT, Norman, OK, and Minneapolis, MN. We had developed life-long friendships in each of those locations. However, the busyness of life prevented us from getting together with many of those friends.

Georg, and her husband, KC, were among those friends. Georg wrote on her Facebook page:

[October 9, 2014]

Old friendships never cease to amaze me. We began our friendship many years ago at Bethany. Although time, kids, jobs, etc., have separated us, and we haven't gotten together often, it was like no time had passed when we saw you Tuesday. We love you guys. Thank you for your hospitality and your inspiring words. We can't wait to see you again.

After that time, we were able to connect with Georg and KC with increased regularity. There were many such special people in our lives. Our resurrected friendships became a great blessing to Becky and me!

I'd be remiss by not adding this final comment. In the introductory chapter of this book, I mentioned that Becky and a friend were feeling a little flirty after the choir concert and decided to introduce themselves to me and my friend. Georg was that friend who was with Becky at that time! She was there the moment I first met Becky!

[October 18, 2014]

Dear Friends,

I am already finishing up the first week of chemo cycle three. Because God continues to bless me with normal days, the days and weeks are passing by quickly in the classroom and with family and friends. Based on cycle two, it was nice to be able to anticipate how the first week would play out. My normal days were Tuesday through Thursday with side effects kicking in Thursday night though Saturday morning. In the busyness of normal, sometimes it's easy to forget that I have cancer! My down days, however, bring me back to reality. I have cancer.

Cancer is a harsh word. I find myself shaking my head at the reality of the diagnosis, especially when I say the words out loud. "I have ovarian cancer." Tears well up when my three-year-old grandson asks, "Grandma, did the medicine make your cancer go away?" I respond, "Isaac, we don't know yet if the medicine will make the cancer go away." And that's okay.

While I don't like having cancer, I like the fact it has renewed my focus on Jesus. **Hebrews 13:8: Jesus Christ is the same yesterday, today, and forever.** These words kept running through my head yesterday during my down day after chemo. Jesus is an unchangeable force in my world of ups and downs. The word cancer previews the harsh reality of sin and death. The name Jesus is the sweet whispered promise of life – life forever in heaven with my Savior.

> How sweet the name of Jesus sounds
> In a believer's ear!
> It soothes his sorrow, heals his wounds,
> And drives away his fear.
>
> It makes the wounded spirit whole,
> And calms the heart's unrest;
> 'Tis manna to the hungry soul,
> And to the weary rest.
>
> Dear name! The Rock on which we build;
> Our shield and hiding place;
> Our never-failing treasury,
> Filled with boundless stores of grace. **(CW 358:1-3)**

Becky's blood test prior to her third infusion was just as good as the prior test. Her CA-125 number decreased from 81 to 17, again by more than a factor of three, still showing the cancer to be chemo-sensitive. These numbers supported the chance she might have a lengthy period of remission and a longer life expectancy. Additionally, at 17, this put her well into the normal range for the test. This was a great sign that the active cancer was being knocked back by the chemo. Except for the impact of the chemo on her system, she didn't feel the cancer symptoms any more. What an incredible blessing!

In the meantime, Becky continued to receive amazing support from her Luther High School family. One of her teaching colleagues is a hockey fan who attended a Minnesota Wild game on October 23, 2014. The game promotion was to fight cancer, and fans were invited to take a sign and write in the name of someone they know who is dealing with cancer.

The picture was captured by Marshall, one of Becky's students, who happened to be watching the game on TV. At one point, the live camera caught her colleague, Jim, holding up the sign with Becky's name on it. Marshall recognized Jim, along with Becky's name on the sign. I'm guessing Marshall had the game on DVR, captured the picture from the DVR playback and shared it on social media. Regardless how he did it, Becky was incredibly honored and very thankful to both Jim and Marshall.

[October 23, 2014]

This is my Luther colleague, Jim Rupprecht, at a Wild game. One of my former students saw this on TV and snapped a photo. Thanks, Jim and Marshall!

Given her experience with breast cancer years earlier, Becky's second cancer occurrence was a red flag for her doctors. Additionally, when breast and ovarian cancer occur in the same person, it suggests the possibility of a genetic influence. After her ovarian cancer diagnosis, we were referred to a geneticist. We eventually learned through a DNA test that Becky was positive for the BRCA2 gene mutation, which has been shown to increase the incidence of breast and ovarian cancers in women. Knowing that, the geneticist suggested our daughters also get tested for that mutation, as it could have been passed on to them. We learned the results in late October.

[October 30, 2014]

Dear Friends,

Because I developed both breast and ovarian cancer, I was tested for the BRCA gene mutation, which greatly increases the odds of developing one or both of these cancers. I tested positive for BRCA2 which explains why I developed both cancers. As a carrier of this gene mutation, there is a 50% chance that I have passed it on to my children. There are many things that I would like to pass on to my children. This is not one of them! However, you will see from Karyn's post below that I did pass this gene mutation on to her. As you read her post, you will also see that while I did pass this gene mutation to her, more importantly, I passed on the hope and faith I have in Jesus.

How thankful I am that Karyn finds her strength and comfort in our loving God and Savior. "My hope is built on nothing less than Jesus' blood and righteousness!"

Our daughter, Karyn, shared her perspective in this post that Becky referenced above:

[October 30, 2014]

A couple of days ago I got a phone call from my genetics counselor, who reported that I tested positive for the BRCA2 gene mutation. This particular mutation is associated with an increased risk for both breast and ovarian cancers, which explains why my dear mother, who also has the mutation, has been diagnosed with both in her relatively young life. While this was not the news we were hoping for, we also know that the course of my life is in the hands of a wise and gracious God. This gene mutation does not mean there is a 100% chance that I will get breast and/or ovarian cancer, but it does increase the odds by four to six times. It also means that each of my children has a 50% chance of inheriting the mutation. If any of them do, there is a chance of their children inheriting it from them.

While this may seem negative and depressing, there are some positive things that could come from having this knowledge. First, you turn to your Maker for comfort and guidance, trusting His will in all things. Second, your health and your time, especially with your family, become even more precious. Third, you have the advantage of knowing that you need to be proactive in cancer prevention and awareness. It's recommended that a female with the BRCA2 gene mutation start breast cancer screening about 10 years earlier, which for me would be pretty soon. There are also more drastic measures you can take, including surgery to remove the female organs, or preventative chemotherapy. Please pray for our family as we make these decisions over the years. Please also continue to pray for my mom as she undergoes her treatment, and for my siblings as they contemplate getting tested.

Sin has caused devastating effects on our world; cancer is one of them. Thanks be to God for sending a Savior to take care of our most serious genetic mutation, our sinful nature, inherited from our first parents, Adam and Eve. **Psalm 73:26: My flesh and my heart may fail, but God is the strength of my heart and my portion forever.**

We were thankful our daughter Kristin tested negative for the gene mutation. We were also thankful that Karyn now knows she carries the same BRCA2 mutation and will be able to make timely decisions for her health in the future.

Nine short weeks prior to this time, we faced tremendous uncertainty regarding Becky's health. We thought she would be lucky to live another year. Now, as Becky was about to start her fourth chemo infusion, we had great hope. We already knew her cancer was knocked back significantly. We knew her cancer was chemo-sensitive and the research showed that meant she had a much better chance of a longer survival time. And, she was feeling good! We knew if this was God's plan for our lives, then He had more He wanted Becky to do with her life on earth.

In her posts, Becky always wanted to point people to her Savior and give all glory to God. In her life, she also wanted other people to know Jesus as their Savior. Knowing that gave her strength as she faced an uncertain future. She wanted others – friends, family, students and caregivers – to feel that same strength and confidence. Spiritual conversations with her oncologist continued. She didn't always say a lot about those conversations in her Facebook posts, but it seemed we spent as much time talking about religion and faith with our doctor as we did about cancer and Becky's ongoing treatments.

Becky's post following her fourth infusion reflected wonderful news regarding how well the chemo was working.

[November 3, 2014]

Dear Friends,

Thanks be to God who gives us the victory through our Lord Jesus Christ. I thank God daily for my spiritual victory through Christ. Today I am thanking God for a cancer victory. I have completed three cycles of chemo. I'm at the halfway point. Prior to my first chemo infusion on August 29, 2014, I had a PET/CT scan. The scan showed that I had a four cm tumor on my right ovary, several smaller tumors in my abdominal cavity and tumors in my lymph nodes from my neck all the way down to my groin. Diagnosis? Stage 4 ovarian cancer. This past Thursday, October 30, I had a PET/CT scan to evaluate the effectiveness of the chemo after three cycles. Prior to my fourth chemo infusion this morning, Glenn and I met with my chemo doctor. Our spiritual dialogue continued. He then asked, "Do you want to talk about cancer?" We smiled and said, "Of course we do!" He went on to say in his low-key manner, "The PET/CT scan shows no active cancer. You are in complete remission."

We were stunned. I suspected we would see a decrease in cancer activity due to how well I was feeling, but *no* cancer? When we questioned the doctor about the results, he said that complete remission after three cycles of chemo is highly unusual. But, as we know, nothing is impossible with God. God is answering all of our prayers for healing with a resounding "Yes!" My doctor is very pleased with the results. However, he is also realistic about the sneakiness of ovarian cancer. He believes there are still random cancer cells lurking about and at some point, they will rear their ugly heads. The PET/CT scan will only pick up abnormalities of a certain size so not all cancer is seen with the scan.

Therefore, I will continue with my three additional chemo treatments, the goal being to kill as many of these random cancer cells as possible. If my side effects continue to be manageable, I may have two additional chemo treatments for a total of eight. Just more fire power to combat and destroy the lurking cancer cells. Ovarian cancer has a tumor marker called CA125. Normal is less than 35. My number was 513 prior to my first chemo treatment. After the first cycle my number had dropped to 81. After the second cycle my number had dropped to 17. After the third cycle my number had dropped to 9! This is another indication that cancer is not active in my body.

Once chemo treatments are completed, I will meet with my doctor every three months. If the CA125 starts to go up, it's an indication the cancer is becoming active again. For some women, that's within six months; for others it is a year or more. For less than 5% of women, the cancer never returns. My doctor is hopeful that I am a good candidate for a remission of a longer duration due to the effectiveness of the chemo to this point. Optimistic as he sounded, he didn't ascribe a time frame.

So, how do I feel knowing that I am in complete remission? Many adjectives come to mind: thankful, relieved, happy, stunned! Most of all I feel humbled—humbled that God has seen fit to give me more time here on earth to serve Him through my vocations as wife, mother, grandmother, friend, daughter, sister, aunt and teacher! I love living one day at a time and savoring each day with the people I treasure. I don't want to lose that feeling or perspective. I love my renewed attention to personal Bible study and prayer. The more I do it, the more I crave it! I love the fact that cancer has made me less of a perfectionist. What a freeing feeling! Bottom line? Cancer has been a blessing in my life!

Thank you for your continued prayers. Thank God for His blessing of remission! And as before, please pray that I can continue to teach while living with cancer. That is my calling right now and it fills my life with meaning! Please pray for my family. Finally, pray that God will be glorified through my cancer journey. **Thanks be to God who gives us the victory through our Lord Jesus Christ!**

It was at this point where we felt real hope that Becky would not only be able to continue teaching for an extended period of time but might be a candidate for a very lengthy remission, if not a cure. I remember wondering if it might be possible that she could beat stage 4 ovarian cancer much like she beat breast cancer. What an amazing turnaround that was for us. We started feeling as though our lives were getting back to normal. I know that was about the time I stopped walking around with my emotions just under the surface. Aside from the fact that Becky still had to go through three more chemo treatments, we started thinking about and planning for a potentially longer life together once again. Even so, I don't think this change ever caused us to lose the appreciation for our time together, though I admit the intensity of our relationship diminished a bit as we settled into a more normal routine. We didn't know what God had planned for us, but it was nice to feel normal again!

[November 23, 2014]

Dear Friends,

Thanksgiving is just around the corner. My dad, a retired pastor, used to say that once a year at Thanksgiving time, his sermon would focus on earthly blessings rather than on spiritual matters. I am going to follow my dad's lead on this one as I reflect on the earthly blessings that have come to me by way of cancer.

- I am thankful I live in a community with top-notch cancer treatment facilities just 15 minutes from home.
- I am thankful for my team of health-care providers.
- I am thankful for health insurance and a wonderful husband who coordinates all the financial details related to my cancer treatment.
- I am thankful for the American Cancer Society. The ACS gives a free wig to all women who lose their hair as a result of cancer treatment. I love my wig! Today as I ventured out into a misty rainy morning, I thought to myself, "If I had my real hair, it would look pretty yucky." My wig held up great under those wet conditions!
- I am thankful for a program called Look Good, Feel Better. LGFB is a non-medical, brand-neutral public service program that teaches beauty techniques to cancer patients to help them manage the appearance-related side effects of cancer treatment. Two weeks ago, I attended a two-hour LGFB class with eight other women who are going through cancer treatment. We had a chance to let our hair down, pun intended, and talk about hair loss, which in many cases includes eyebrows and eyelashes, as well as skin issues related to chemo and radiation. Best of all we all went away with a bag full of skin care products and make-up that were donated by a variety of cosmetic companies. My favorite was an eyebrow pencil and brush. Our LGFB teacher showed me how to shape natural-looking eyebrows around the few stray lashes that remain on my brow.
- I am thankful for Maid Like New and Cleaning for a Reason. Friends of ours gave us a gift certificate for a house cleaning through the La Crosse company, Maid Like New. What a treat to come home to a truly clean house two weeks ago!
- I am thankful for the YMCA program, LIVESTRONG. Livestrong is a 12-week small-group fitness program for adult cancer survivors who want to regain their health and well-being. I have not participated in this program to date,

but look forward to participating in one of the future sessions.

- I am thankful for all of the generous companies and individuals who have touched my life and the lives of my cancer counterparts as we travel along our cancer journey. Your kindness is very much appreciated! I look forward to paying it forward in some way that will make a difference in the lives of those living with cancer.

Tomorrow is my fifth chemo infusion. Thank you for your continued prayers on my behalf. May you all have a blessed Thanksgiving!

We praise you, O God, our Redeemer, Creator;
In grateful devotion our tribute we bring;
We lay it before you; we kneel and adore you;
We bless your holy name: glad praises we sing. **(CW 609:1)**

There is nothing like a cancer remission to help us focus on all the wonderful people and programs that have been created to help cancer patients on their journey. This post highlights the ones that specifically touched our lives as Becky went through her journey during the first few months. It was humbling to be shown such love from so many different people and groups. As if we didn't already appreciate all those blessings, adding Thanksgiving to that mix really provided an opportunity to reflect and be incredibly thankful!

Becky and I, along with our son Ryan, were invited to our friends' home for a Thanksgiving dinner. They had a tablecloth on the table which they had used for a number of years. On it, those present wrote things that they were thankful for at that time. That year, we were invited to do so as well. I don't remember what Becky and I wrote, but I remember Ryan was thankful for chemo and modern medicine. It was clear at that time the chemo was a blessing in our lives and we would be blessed that ovarian cancer, at least in Becky's case, would not win just yet!

[December 3, 2014]

Dear friends,

Even though we have never met, Lisa Vogel Rittierodt is my Facebook friend, my sister in Christ and my sister in ovarian cancer. Lisa reached out to me via Facebook when she noticed teal cancer ribbons dancing around my status this past August. It turns out that Lisa and I share mutual friends. She lives in Washington not too far from Kristin and Pete, and her pastor is the son of my best friend from high school.

I am indebted to Lisa for holding my cyber hand through my initial diagnosis and my first weeks of chemo. She counseled me on what to eat and what not to eat, laxatives, suppositories and all that fun stuff that comes with pumping your body full of poison. I had an open invitation to text, email or message her day or night, and I took her up on that offer. Most importantly, we encouraged each other with the promises that our gracious God gives us in His Word.

Lisa has now learned that after five-and-a-half years of living with ovarian cancer, her options for treatment have been exhausted. She is on the last leg of her earthly journey with her eyes fixed on Jesus and the prize of heaven.

Lisa, I want you to know how much I have appreciated the help you have given me in my walk with cancer. I continue to walk with you as you finish the race.

> I walk with Jesus all the way,
> His guidance never fails me;
> Within His wounds I find a stay
> When Satan's power assails me;
> And by His footsteps led,
> My path I safely tread.
> In spite of ills that threaten may,
> I walk with Jesus all the way.
>
> My walk is heavenward all the way;
> Await my soul, the morrow,
> When thou shalt find release for aye
> From all thy sin and sorrow.
> All worldly pomp, be gone!
> To heaven I now press on.
> For all the world I would not stay;
> My walk is heavenward all the way. **(ELH 252:5-6)**

Lisa's online blog post follows:

When I was diagnosed with ovarian cancer, I knew I would learn many things. I also thought I would be healed in a short amount of time. That hasn't been God's plan for me. But in that time, I have learned so many things that I want to start sharing with others in the hope that through my walk with ovarian cancer and with God I can help others through their struggles. To God be the Glory!

My Race is Almost Run

Running has never been a favorite pastime of mine. I remember having to run a mile every day in grade school. Even during basketball season I could never run the entire mile without stopping.

The distance was always too long. Now it seems that a lengthy earthly race will also be too long for me.

My oncologist confirmed what Paul and I have been suspecting for the last week. I am out of options. I cannot take the oral medication because I won't be able to absorb the benefits due to my g-tube. Also, we will never know if it is the medication that is causing my issues or my digestive tract problems. She did look quickly to see if there were any trials, but those are very hard to get into even in the best of circumstances.

Paul and I had a good talk with Dr. Swisher and my nurse, Holly. They said it was up to me to keep trying different treatments in hopes of extending my life or to do something else that would give me a better quality of life. Either way there is no guarantees of anything.

Right now my main focus is getting to Disneyland at the end of the month. The Dream Foundation is working with us and something should be done soon. We are going either way because our trip is already paid for. Hopefully they can get us the extra medical support I will need for traveling and for the time at Disney. We know quite a bit of paperwork has come across my doctor's desk so things are moving forward.

After that I will be going back on Avastin, a drug that I was on before. It took my ascites away and the hope is that it might keep the cancer stable for a time. Once again, there is no guarantee.

As far as a timeline, they really can't give me one. Just like with my mom, all of a sudden things will shut down. What they did say is that it's not weeks but it's not years. I asked about my family reunion in July and both my doctor and my nurse said that it's unlikely that I will be able to travel then. They did say that it could be different in two to three months when they see how things are going on Avastin.

We will cross that bridge with the rest of the family when we come to it.

We told the kids on Monday. Please pray for them. It's not easy hearing that your mom will be going home to heaven before you are even close to being an adult. They all reacted differently but how we expected. Melanie chose to stay home with me yesterday where the boys decided to go to school. Pray for Melanie as she sees her friends and lets them know. That is going to be hard for her. Pray for the boys as they process things in their own way. Pray for them to open up when they need to.

Please pray for Paul. He already is doing the jobs of both parents since I am quite limited. He's getting tired and is always in need of help with rides or things around the house. We appreciate any help people can give us.

As I have been pondering the past few days, the verse Melanie chose as her confirmation verse kept running through my mind. **1 Corinthians 9:24: Do you not know that in a race all the runners run, but only one gets the prize? Run in such a way as to get the prize.**

For a long time, I have pictured my race as something like this:

Like I said before, I've never liked running. My thought of this verse was the hard pounding runners endure in their training. Honestly, that is part of our spiritual running, isn't it? We have to pound away, constantly learning, constantly training to keep God's Word embedded in our hearts. But now, I'm looking at the verse like this:

Do you not know that in a race all the runners run, but only one gets the prize? Run in such a way as to get the prize 1 Corinthians 9:24

This is a painting Melanie's first grade teacher made for her

confirmation. It's based on 1 Corinthians 9:24. I love this because it's a child. A child just keeps running because that's what children do. That child knows he or she is going to get to the goal, and the goal will be wonderful. There is no hardship, but there is urgency. There is no wondering, yet there is expectation. There is no angst, just joy.

As I finish my race, I am going to run with child-like faith. I know I am running to a beautiful place. The last part of the race won't be easy, but the reward will be amazing.

What a wonderful, faith-filled post from an amazing person we never got to meet. Even so, it is obvious from her post that her experience mirrored ours. She showed Becky a faith-filled path, a path that was so very similar to Becky's.

Lisa was one of Becky's early mentors after Becky was first diagnosed with ovarian cancer. Lisa was a confidant and friend who shared the highs and lows of the ovarian cancer journey with her. God put Lisa in Becky's life at the right time to help her along the way. We were saddened that we never had the chance to connect with Lisa in person.

What strikes me most about Lisa's final blog post are the pictures and Bible passages she included in it. They were much like the pictures Becky loved and the passages Becky focused on in her last months. The image of completing the race. The image of going down a path toward a future that we cannot completely see, but one we know will be fantastic. Lisa and Becky shared much more than ovarian cancer. They shared the same knowledge, belief and confident hope in their future because they knew their Savior!

[December 29, 2014]

Dear Friends,

Four months ago, on August 29, I had my first chemo infusion. A week ago, I had my sixth and final infusion. The first phase of my cancer journey is complete. Going into this journey, I had no idea what to expect. Looking back on this experience I have come to realize that everyone's journey is unique – from the way each person faces the journey, to the chemo side effects, to the chemo outcome.

In my case, I have had the most favorable outcome possible! Manageable side effects allowed me to teach the entire first semester with minimal disruption. After three treatment cycles, scans and blood tests showed that I was in complete remission. God answered your prayers and mine with "Yes!" I am humbled and grateful!

So now what? Phase two begins – a phase called *watchful waiting*. I will be scheduled for scans and blood tests every three months. The first one on January 22 will monitor the overall state of my health. Even though the chemo knocked my cancer into remission, in most cases ovarian cancer recurs at some point. I have decided that I am going to expect that my cancer will recur. That way I won't be surprised if it does recur and I will be thankful for as long as I stay in remission!

And so, I move forward into a new calendar year. I am looking forward to normal days of sharing a glass of wine with Glenn in front of the fire, the birth of two new grandchildren and students that energize me with their Spanish communication. With God's help I want to live each day with purpose in each of my varied roles. I want my cancer journey to continue to bring glory to our God. Thank you, thank you for the countless prayers you have sent heavenward on my behalf. I ask for your continued prayers as I move into this next phase.

> Help us, O Lord, for now we enter
> Upon another year today.
> In you our hopes and thoughts now center;
> Renew our courage for the way.
> New life, new strength, new happiness
> We ask of you -- oh, hear and bless.

May every plan and undertaking
Begin this year, O Lord, with you;
When I am sleeping or am waking,
Help me, dear Lord, your will to do.
In you alone, my God, I live;
You only can my sins forgive.

Jesus, be with me and direct me;
Jesus, my plans and hopes inspire;
Jesus, from tempting thoughts protect me;
Jesus, be all my heart's desire;
Jesus, be in my thoughts all day
And never let me fall away. **(CW 70:1-2,4)**

Chapter 8

Living in Remission – Our Bonus Years

This isn't the definition of bonus years Becky had suggested a couple of years earlier. Bonus years they were, however. At this point, every additional day, month and year was a bonus for us. In January, 2015, that reality was underscored when one of Becky's relatives (and a family friend) was taken home to heaven.

[January 24, 2015]

Dear Friends,

This was a week of death and life, sorrow and joy. On Tuesday, I attended the funeral of my cousin, Mark Harstad. Mark and I were diagnosed with cancer within days of each other this past August. Mark's cancer was a rare and aggressive form of leukemia. God called Mark home to heaven just five months after his diagnosis. He experienced physical death but received eternal life. His family experienced sorrow for the loss but know joy now that he is in heaven. At the funeral we were visibly reminded that the wages of sin is death as Mark's lifeless body lay in the coffin. Pastor Petersen comforted us with the sweet message of the Gospel! **Romans 6:23: But the gift of God is eternal life in Christ Jesus our Lord!**

A new life entered this world on Thursday morning. Abel Charles was born to Mike and Karyn and joins brothers Isaac (4) and Matthias (2) in the Lukasek family. What joy his birth brings to our family! We will witness his new life in Christ as he becomes a child of God through baptism next Sunday.

Thursday was also my follow-up appointment after my last chemo infusion in December. The PET/CT showed that I am still in complete remission. "There is no evidence of disease," my doctor said. Glenn and I were filled with joy and thanksgiving upon hearing this news. My doctor, however, continues to temper the news of remission with the reality that ovarian cancer almost always recurs at some point, most often within two years.

The remission plan is that I will have check-ups every three months to assess my health status. I admit that it's unsettling to have the prospect of recurrence hanging over my head. At the same time, I try not to fret. The apostle Paul put it succinctly: **Philippians 1:21, For to me, to live is Christ and to die is gain.** I have been given the gift of time and God still has work for me to do! And really, this gift of time applies not just to me, but to all of us, whether we are sick or healthy! Each day is a gift of God's grace, and when our time on earth is ended we have a home in heaven with our Savior that He has prepared for us. It doesn't get any better than that!

Glenn and I continue to have spiritual discussions with my doctor as he searches for the truth. Please pray that the Holy Spirit will work faith in his heart through hearing and reading that his sins are forgiven through Jesus. I close with a hymn verse that we sang at Mark's funeral:

Jesus died for my transgression,
All my sins on Him were laid;
Jesus won for me salvation,
On the cross my debt was paid.
From the grave I shall arise
And shall meet Him in the skies.
Death itself is transitory;
I shall lift my head in glory! **(ELH 354:5)**

Becky mentioned in her post that Mark had a rare form of cancer. It never really struck me at the time, but I have since learned that whenever someone has a rare form of cancer, it is usually an indicator that an earthly prognosis will not be good. Ovarian cancer, pancreatic cancer and others are not rare, but they are problematic because most people don't know they have them until it is too late. On the other hand, rare forms of cancer are frequently misdiagnosed and, even when diagnosed correctly, the doctors don't have a lot of good treatment options because of the more limited research that is done on those types of cancer.

Mark's death was surreal for us. When he and Becky were diagnosed at the same time, they connected even more closely as both relatives and friends. They called themselves the cancer cousins. It felt a little unfair that we should be doing so well at that time while Mark was failing. It felt like we could very well have also been in that position had Becky's cancer not been chemo-sensitive. We didn't know what God had in store for us, but we were once again reminded to be thankful for the blessings we had!

[April 25, 2015]

Dear Friends,

Lamentations 3:22-23: The steadfast love of the Lord never ceases; his mercies never come to an end; they are new every morning. My heart is singing this song from Lamentations as I share with you the news from my three-month check-up this past Thursday. I continue to be in remission! My cancer number (CA-125) remains at five which is well within the normal range. Until that number makes a significant jump, the doctor said there is little reason to suspect that the cancer is waking up. Living in remission has given me the opportunity to reflect on a number of things about cancer and about life and death as a Christian. Below are some of my musings:

WAITING AND WONDERING – While I was undergoing chemo treatment, I knew that chemo was knocking back the cancer. Once the chemo ended, the waiting and wondering began. I am not a worrier by nature, but these past three months I have found myself wondering if little twinges in my pelvis or abdominal gas and pressure were signs the cancer was returning. My doctor explained on Thursday that an elevated CA-125 will most likely be the first indication that the cancer has returned. Symptoms will then follow. While I know in my head and heart that I don't need to worry about this or anything else, anxieties in my sub-conscious manifest themselves in an uneasiness which ramped up the week before my blood test. These feelings disappeared just as quickly after I got the results from my blood tests. My new normal will be broken up into three-month chunks of waiting and wondering, but I don't want that to define my days. It's unbelievable how the peace of God that surpasses all understanding calms my troubled heart and fills me with joy to live each day as fully as I can.

Cancer is unsettling but my sins are even more unsettling. Thankfully I never have to wait and wonder if my sins are forgiven. Jesus' perfect righteousness covers them all. God has declared me holy through Christ! So, if there's any waiting and wondering to be done, it's this: when will heaven be my home and how wonderful will it be?

HAIR – My hair is growing back. For months now, I have been reminded of my mortality every time I looked in the mirror and saw my bald head. I had a bald head because I have cancer. Cancer kills the body. Someday I will die. More recently when I look in the mirror I am reminded of new life. My hair is starting to grow back. I have eyelashes that are beginning to peek out of my lids. New life! What a blessing God has given me in my body! I exclaim with King David, **I am fearfully and wonderfully made!** It's been fascinating to watch my hair grow back, to see what my hairline looks like, to feel the softness of new hair and to see the pretty swirls and natural growth pattern. Losing my hair was not a big deal for me since I never really liked my hair in the first place! I have loved my wig – the style, the color, and of course, all the wonderful compliments I have received. I felt pretty during a time when there was an ugly sickness coursing through me. I have to admit that I am a little self-conscious about sporting my new pixie-look in public. But it's time! My real hair is starting to peek out from under the wig.

HAVING AN ACTION PLAN – In September of 2012, a former Luther dad was diagnosed with cancer. Karl was just a couple years younger than me. I was stunned when I heard the news and prayed fervently that God would restore him to health. Instead, God's plan was to bring him home to heaven. During the eight months of life that God granted Karl after his diagnosis, he joyfully proclaimed Jesus to his family and friends, to his healthcare providers, to his co-workers and to me!

Karl inspired me. Glenn remembers me saying as we drove to Karl's funeral, "If someday I am diagnosed again with cancer, I want to be like Karl." By that I meant, I want to find joy in my circumstances, I want to cling to the confidence that comes from knowing that I am a redeemed child of God, and I want to share that joy and hope with others. I had an action plan.

Having an action plan has helped me navigate the choppy waters of cancer. With God's guidance, I have been proactive rather than reactive in my response to the diagnosis, the treatment and now remission. I don't know if my remission will last another six months or 20 years, but I am confident that my heavenly Father will be by my side as I continue to journey through life and live with cancer. I love God's action plan spelled out for us in **Isaiah 43:1,3: Do not fear, for I have redeemed you; I have called you by name; you are mine! For I am the LORD your God, The Holy One of Israel, your Savior.**

In early May, Becky was approaching the end of the school year. What an unbelievable year it had been, including her initial diagnosis, all the incredible support she received, the blessings and challenges of her treatments, and the opportunity to have a second semester in complete remission. Aside from thankfulness to God, Becky was incredibly thankful to all of her school friends and colleagues for their support throughout the year. This is the letter she wrote to them:

[May 12, 2015]

Dear friends of Luther High School,

On Friday, August 1, 2014, I had a lump in my groin biopsied. Results were expected the following Tuesday. I went to bed a bit anxious Monday evening. I woke up in the middle of the night with these words running through my mind: God is our refuge and strength, an ever-present help in trouble. Tuesday afternoon, our in-service opened with a devotion based on **Psalm 46: God is our refuge and strength**, the very same words of comfort from the night before! I had no idea this verse came from Psalm 46, nor did I realize our theme for the school year was also found in **Psalm 46: Be still and know that I am God**. In my mind, this was no coincidence, but rather God's way of calming me even before I received my cancer diagnosis three days later.

I want to thank you, friends of Luther High School, for your prayerful support throughout this past school year. With the encouragement of many, I decided to attempt to teach while undergoing chemo treatments. God graciously answered the prayers of many by blessing me with the most positive chemo response possible: manageable side effects and complete remission. Please thank God with me for this blessing. It's been a wonderful and memorable school year!

My prayer now is that God will continue to hold the cancer at bay so I can teach for another year. I ask for your prayers that God's will for me will allow this desire to happen.

Lamentations 3:22-23: The steadfast love of the Lord never ceases; his mercies never come to an end; they are new every morning; great is your faithfulness!

In His service,

Becky Lussky

She followed that letter with this Facebook post when the school year officially ended.

[May 22, 2015]

Dear Friends,

Yesterday marked the end of my 20th year of teaching at Luther High School. In August, 1995, I was called as an emergency part-time teacher when Jim Raabe, Luther's principal and Spanish teacher, was killed in a car accident three weeks before school started. I was 35 years old, young and full of energy and enthusiasm! I had 25 students divided between one Spanish 1 class and one Spanish 2 class. I was relatively fluent in Spanish after four years of high school Spanish, a summer in Nicaragua and a year in Peru as a mission volunteer. I also had graduated from college with a minor in Spanish, but I had no clue how to teach the language. Two weeks before school started, I was handed a key to Dr. Raabe's classroom and left alone to figure things out! My German counterpart at Luther, Kurt Wittmershaus, befriended me and mentored me.

Early on I connected with the Wisconsin Association of Foreign Language Teachers (WAFLT). I still regularly attend the annual WAFLT fall conferences and summer institutes where I network with other teachers and glean teaching strategies from the excellent workshops. More recently, my mentor has been Prof. Paul Bases at MLC, who encouraged me to become a target-language teacher which means that all instruction and all student interaction is conducted in Spanish. I resisted this concept at first. I didn't believe I was fluent enough to teach in Spanish, but four years ago I decided to take the target-language plunge and I have never looked back! I am also indebted to my three MLC student teachers who introduced me to Spanish-language films and brought new and innovative ideas into my classroom.

Here I am, 20 years later. I am now 56 years old, not quite as young or energetic, but still filled with plenty of enthusiasm. I teach six hours a day with 136 students divided between Spanish 1, Spanish 2 and Spanish 3 classes. I still struggle with feeling inadequate as a Spanish teacher, especially in regard to my oral fluency, but it's obvious to me that God put me in this role 20 years ago, and He's not ready for me to relinquish it just yet.

This past year has been especially sweet. When I was diagnosed with cancer the week before school started, it appeared to be God's way of saying my time as a teacher had come to an end. Instead, it was His way of drawing me closer to Him through His Word while still allowing me to teach. How awesome is that! I am so thankful that God answered my prayers and your prayers on my behalf with, "Yes! Continue to teach!" As I close out my 20th year, I am humbled by the immeasurable blessings that God has showered upon me and my dear students. My specific prayer request is that I will be able to teach another year. I ask for your continued prayers and encouragement. **1 Corinthians 15:57: Thanks be to God who gives us the victory through our Lord Jesus Christ.** To God be the glory!

Becky's transformation from her pre-breast cancer days to this point in her life was nothing short of a miracle. She went from someone who wasn't sure she had the energy to teach any more to someone who absolutely loved time in the classroom with her students. Part of this change was going to target-language teaching. Part of it was her feeling re-energized as God guided her through her two cancers.

Most people hold a variety of personal viewpoints on different subjects. While we know what we know, we don't always know what we don't know. In other words, we may not be aware there are other perspectives to consider that would help us in our lives and vocations. Becky held perspectives and opinions about a lot of things. In my opinion, she was well-informed and on target most of the time. Still, she was always open to learning about new ideas and trying new things, especially when it came to her role as a teacher. She was well-liked by her students, but she didn't always understand or appreciate the difference between *doing* things for her students and *being* there for her students. She reflected on that in a personal white paper immediately after the school year concluded. I'm not sure she ever shared this with anyone, but the lessons she learned from her reading and from her colleagues had an impact on her perspective. She had a renewed appreciation for the need to find the right balance between *doing* and *being.*

REFLECTIONS ON TEACHING
June 4, 2015

I am cleaning out files and came across an article I read on Facebook called *What Students Remember Most About Teachers.* The article, which I'll include following my comments, struck a chord with me for several reasons.

For years, I saw myself as the young teacher down the hall, even though I am now an older, veteran teacher. I was always busy *doing.* I wanted my lessons to be interesting and my PowerPoints to be engaging, so I spent long hours trying to perfect these things. At the end of the day, I often felt I hadn't achieved the perfection I was striving for. I would go at it again the next day, always wondering if what I was doing as a teacher was good enough. Ironically, students sometimes got in the way of my quest to be the best teacher. During my prep periods, I worked feverishly to tweak and hone the lessons for my next class period or the next day. When students stopped by to chat or ask questions, I dropped what I was doing to be there for them, but inside I had to push aside thoughts that I was losing valuable prep time!

I wasn't aware I was like this until several years ago. We were having a discussion in a faculty meeting regarding the number of students frequently absent from homeroom doing other activities. Some teachers wanted those students in homeroom so they could have more time to connect with them. I thought to myself, "I would love to have the students gone from homeroom so I could get more work done!" It dawned on me that these other teachers were wired differently than me. They were looking for more opportunities to enhance their personal connections with the students. Conversely, while I appreciated the personal student connections, I also felt there were times when their needs were an obstacle to getting my work done. I decided I wanted to be more like my colleagues by trying to put relationships first. I naturally want to *do* rather than *be*, so I now consciously try to find a better balance between *doing* and *being*.

In February 2014, I was honored as WKBT-TV's Top Notch Teacher, a monthly award given to local educators in the area. What a humbling honor for someone who always wondered if what she was doing as a teacher was good enough! One of my Spanish students named Lilli, along with her mother, had nominated me for this recognition. I remained in my classroom while Lilli was interviewed by the reporter. I was struck by the fact that Lilli never once mentioned that she thought I was a great teacher or that my PowerPoint presentations were interesting or that my classes inspired her to continue studying Spanish in college. Instead, she talked about me as a person. She told the reporter that I was caring, a Christian role model, and someone she looked up to. Really? That wasn't a part of my lesson plans! Thankfully, the traits Lilli mentioned did manifest themselves in my life even though I wasn't consciously trying to model them. Thankfully, God had been using me not just as a Spanish teacher, but also as a Christian woman who cared for and loved her students. Being a well-prepared teacher is important, but my prayer is that I can meet my students' needs on many different levels – spiritually, emotionally and academically.

What I learned from this experience is that it's not about Spanish. Teaching is about personal relationships, and, most importantly, the personal relationship God has established with each of us through Jesus!

WHAT STUDENTS REMEMBER MOST
ABOUT TEACHERS
Posted January 26, 2014 by Pursuit of a Joyful Life

Dear Young Teacher Down the Hall,

I saw you as you rushed past me in the lunchroom. Urgent. In a hurry to catch a bite before the final bell would ring calling all the students back inside. I noticed that your eyes showed tension. There were faint creases in your forehead. I asked you how your day was going and you sighed.

"Oh, fine," you replied.

I knew it was anything but fine. I noticed the stress was getting to you. I could tell the pressure was rising. I looked at you and made an intentional decision to stop you right then and there. To ask you how things were really going. Was it that I saw in you a glimpse of myself that made me take the moment?

You told me how busy you were, how much there was to do. How little time there was to get it all done. I listened. And then I told you this: I told you to remember that at the end of the day, it's not just about lesson plans. It's not about the fancy stuff we teachers make — the crafts we do, the stories we read, the papers we laminate. No, that's not really it. That's not what matters most.

As I looked at you there wearing all that worry under all that strain, I said it's about being there for your kids. When it's all said and done, most students won't remember what amazing lesson plans you created. They won't remember how organized your bulletin boards were or how straight your rows of desks were.

But they will remember you.

Your kindness. Your empathy. Your care and concern. They'll remember that you took the time to listen. That you stopped to ask them how they were. They'll remember the personal stories you told about your life, your home, your pets, your kids. They'll remember your laugh. They'll remember that you sat and talked with them while they ate lunch.

What really matters is YOU. You are that difference in their lives.

I looked at you as tears welled up in your eyes, emotions rising to the surface. I told you gently to stop trying so hard. I reminded you that your own expectations were causing all your stress. Those of us who truly care are often harder on ourselves than our students are willing to be. Those of us who truly care are often our own worst enemies. We beat ourselves up for trivial failures. We tell ourselves we're not good enough. We compare ourselves to others. We work ourselves to the bone in hopes of achieving the perfect lesson plans, the most dynamic activities, the most engaging lectures.

Why? Because we want our students to think we're the best at what we do. We believe that excellence is achieved by doing. What we often forget is that excellence is more readily attained by being.

Being available.
Being kind.
Being compassionate.
Being transparent.
Being thoughtful.

Kids can see through to the truth of the matter. Flashy stuff can entertain them for a while, but it's the constancy of empathy that keeps them connected to us. It's the relationships we build with them. It's the time we invest. It's all the little ways we stop and show concern. It's the love we share with them – love of learning, love of life and love of people.

While we continually strive for excellence in our profession, we need to remember one simple truth. It's the human touch that matters most. It's you, their teacher, that matters most!

Go back to your classroom and really take a look. See past the behavior of your students and other pressing concerns. Look beyond the stack of papers on your desk and the backlog of emails in your inbox. Look beyond the classrooms of seasoned teachers down the hall. Look, and you will see that it's there right inside you. You have the ability to make an impact. You have the chance of a lifetime to make a difference in a child's life. Right where you are, just as you are.

Fondly,

That Other Teacher Down the Hall

Following is the WKBT-TV Top Notch Teacher story from February, 2014.

February Top Notch Teacher: Becky Lussky
Luther High School Spanish teacher and mentor to students

ONALASKA, Wis. (WKBT) - February's Top Notch Teacher comes from Luther High School in Onalaska. Becky Lussky is known for creating upbeat lesson plans and activities in her Spanish class, as well as being a role model for her students.

"The first day they walk into my classroom, they are greeted in Spanish, and we never go backwards," Lussky said.

She's been a teacher at Luther High for almost two decades.

"I have a passion for the language, and it's fun to impart that passion to the students."

Lussky said the best thing about her job is seeing her students use the language outside the classroom.

"For example, students will come to me and say, 'Senora, yesterday at work I was able to help a Spanish speaking customer.'"

This brings her one step closer to her goal.

"My number one goal for my students is that they have the confidence to communicate in Spanish."

Teaching Spanish is just part of her job. The other part is being a mentor.

"One of our goals as teachers is to prepare our students to be productive citizens," Lussky said.

That is why she is the advisor for the National Honor Society.

"She encourages us to help the community and help other people as best we can," said Luther High School student Lilli Gannon.

Gannon, a member of the National Honor Society, looks up to Mrs. Lussky as a leader.

"She lets her light shine in all she does and she's a great example of a Christian woman," Gannon said.

Leading by example for the students she cares so much about, Mrs. Lussky is more than just a teacher.

"I have a passion for teaching which comes from loving my students," Lussky said.

Mrs. Lussky is in her 19th year of teaching at Luther High School and will continue to spread her passion for language to her students.

The summer of 2015 was certainly special. Becky was in full remission and feeling good. She exercised daily and was conscious of eating well. She loved her time at our cabin, where she was able to relax, ski, and have fun with her grandchildren! There was much for which to be thankful, and I think we all appreciated it even more because of the cancer.

Along with our daughters, Becky's younger sister Liz was also tested for the BRCA2 gene mutation, since she also had a 50% chance of having that gene passed down to her. She learned shortly thereafter from her doctor that she did indeed have the mutation. She opted to be proactive to prevent any cancer occurrence. During that process, her doctors were amazed to find that she had ovarian cancer in its earliest stage. If my recollection is correct, the story we were told is that this might be one of the earliest findings of ovarian cancer ever identified.

What a blessing it was they found Liz's cancer when they did. It was all because of the genetic testing process that was initiated due to Becky's two cancer occurrences.

[August 12, 2015]

Dear Friends,

Today marks the one-year anniversary of my cancer diagnosis. Unbelievable! This past week, as I blocked out my courses for this upcoming school year, I looked back at my lesson plans from last year. "Chemo - Gail here" dotted my first semester plans. A year ago, I set out to teach while being treated with chemo. I had no point of reference. Yes, I had heard chemo horror stories, but I didn't have the experiences of a close personal friend or family member to reference. Therefore, I somewhat naively set out on this new journey. My chemo journey was as smooth as anyone's could be. I experienced manageable, tolerable side effects which did not derail my teaching nor interfere much with my personal life.

While I was very thankful that my chemo experience was so positive, I didn't truly appreciate what a gift it was until my younger sister Liz was diagnosed with ovarian cancer this past May. Liz and I are very close. Over the years we have always shared our joys and sorrows with each other. However, a cancer experience was *not* something that I wanted to share with her! God had different plans.

Because I tested positive for the BRCA2 gene mutation, there was a 50% chance my siblings would also test positive. Sure enough, Liz tested positive! Testing positive may appear to be a negative result, but in Liz's case it was a huge blessing. Since there is no screening for ovarian cancer, Liz decided to have prophylactic surgery, a procedure meant to prevent disease. Here's where the blessing part comes in. Her ovaries and fallopian tubes were removed and tested following surgery, revealing that Liz already had early-stage ovarian cancer! From all indications, the cancer was removed with surgery, but as an additional preventative measure, it was recommended that surgery be followed by three rounds of chemo. "No problem," thought Liz, "Becky sailed through chemo just fine." Unfortunately, that was not to be the case for my dear sister. She has had every awful side effect possible, some lasting for days, others for weeks, right up to the next infusion.

It fascinates me that sisters with the same disease and the same treatment have had such different responses to treatment. I look back on my chemo journey with a renewed awe, humbled over and over again by God's goodness to me. I would never have been able to teach had I experienced the severe side effects Liz experienced. Not surprisingly, Liz also speaks of God's goodness to her through cancer and chemo. While this has been an extremely difficult experience physically, she sees blessings wherever she turns – incredible spiritual strengthening, the love and compassion shown to her by her husband and sons, the kindness of friends and church family and the support from her co-workers.

Yesterday was Liz's third and final chemo infusion. I pray that this medical intervention has successfully eradicated the cancer. I had my three-month check-up in July and I'm so thankful that I continue to be in remission. As such, I am excitedly gearing up for another school year.

Liz and I are sisters who now share a cancer journey; more importantly, we share the blessings of a faith anchored in our Savior, Jesus Christ. Thank you for your continued encouragement and prayers on our behalf. **Isaiah 40:31: But those who hope in the Lord will renew their strength. They will soar on wings like eagles; they will run and not grow weary, they will walk and not be faint.** To God be the glory!

A part of the blessing of remission was feeling good. And Becky was feeling good. She had a lot of energy. Anyone who looked at her on a day to day basis would never know she was dealing with stage 4 ovarian cancer. Life felt normal once again. We worked, got together with friends, went to events together, and spent time with our family, all the normal things people do. One of the fun events we attended in September, 2015, was a "Steampunk" wedding. The bride and groom decided that was the theme they wanted, and all those attending were invited to dress up in Steampunk style. Life as a drama costumer has its perks, so Becky was

able to find some appropriate threads for us. I felt pretty stylish and well within the norm at the wedding, but in my mind, Becky looked fabulous.

Less than a week later, we celebrated our 32nd anniversary. I wrote: "32 years ago this day, I married my best friend. She's still my best friend. God has surely blessed us during these years together. Very thankful!" Becky wrote: "This is what 32 years of marriage looks like: a wonderful husband and seven beautiful grandchildren. Our wedding text says it all.

Psalm 136:1: O Give thanks unto the Lord, for He is good; for His mercy endures forever.

I always enjoyed going to events with my lovely wife. Every year in December, the Lussky side of our family had a Christmas get-together at a show in the Twin Cities. Usually, it was at the Chanhassen Dinner Theater. In December, 2015, we attended *A Christmas Carol* at the Guthrie Theater in downtown Minneapolis. Becky posted this photo, taken outside the atrium overlook.

We were certainly enjoying being together and living out our bonus years. But that picture and those feelings belied some of the anxiety that lurked beneath the surface. It had been almost a full year since Becky had finished her chemo, and over 13 months since she had been declared to be in complete remission. We knew the cancer could come back at any time, and that did cause some anxiety.

In her cancer journal, Becky wrote about how she felt a day before our Christmas outing with our family. She didn't share this on Facebook. I think she simply needed to express how she felt in words. In the end, one of the great comforts for her in these times was in God's Word. From this journal entry, you can see how she related to an online post by another woman with cancer. But, more than that, it is evident how she turned those feelings of anxiousness into comfort, knowing that her Heavenly Father has her life securely in His hands, knowing that He will care for all her needs.

[December 11, 2015]

I have been anxious recently, wondering when my cancer will return. I'm hyper-sensitive to physical symptoms like twinges in my abdomen, pelvic pressure and gas, that perhaps indicate a recurrence. Life is going well; I am enjoying time with my family, having a wonderful school year, etc. I don't want this to end. When things are going well, my focus is not on heaven. That's okay, I think, since I am supposed to be living my life here on earth. Throughout this journey, I have come to appreciate each day as a gift. I don't want to worry about the future, but Satan and my sinful nature are doing battle with me. I want to find a balance between living a full life while God gives me the gift of time. At the same time, I long for heaven. Sometimes it's a hard balance to find! This morning I pulled up a blog post by Kara Tippets, a woman who died of breast cancer earlier this year. She really nailed how I'm feeling!

Matthew 6:25-34: Therefore I tell you, do not worry about your life, what you will eat or drink; or about your body, what you will wear. Is not life more than food, and the body more than clothes? Look at the birds of the air; they do not sow or reap or store away in barns, and yet your heavenly Father feeds them. Are you not much more valuable than they? Can any one of you by worrying add a single hour to your life? And why do you worry about clothes? See how the flowers of the field grow. They do not labor or spin. Yet I tell you that not even Solomon in all his splendor was dressed like one of these. If that is how God clothes the grass of the field, which is here today and tomorrow is thrown into the fire, will he not much more clothe you—you of little faith? So, do not worry, saying, 'What shall we eat?' or 'What shall we drink?' or 'What shall we wear?' For the pagans run after all these things, and your heavenly Father knows that you need them. But seek first his kingdom and his righteousness, and all these things will be given to you as well. Therefore, do not worry about tomorrow, for tomorrow will worry about itself. Each day has enough trouble of its own.

From Kara Tippets' blog post:

I struggle with jealousy in a way I have never experienced in my life. I look at people and long for carefree thinking. I long to be anxious over things like my weight, my kids' behavior, education, politics, the environment, or farming and food production. I never have been much of a worrier, and I rarely struggle with anxiety. Certainly, I experienced these things in the intense moments of life, but not on a regular basis.

Now, my heart is different. Heavier. More focused on each moment. Everything feels intense. I had some mamas laughing yesterday over my overwhelming need to create memories for my kids. Death is a reality for us all, but it was once a distant reality. It has come near. Closer. More certain. I want to wear a banner that says, begs, REMEMBER THIS MOMENT! WE ARE NOT PROMISED OUR NEXT MOMENT. I'M PRESENT IN THIS MOMENT FOR YOU! As one can imagine, it's not a normal place to live. It has its benefits and drawbacks. This kind of living comes with more hugs and kisses, more "I love yous."

I can't just have fun sledding. I want the joyous moment emblazoned on the thoughts of each of my children and husband. The thoughts that will remind them of a mama that had fun. A mama that isn't sick, a mama that was silly. "See me, kids. I'm laughing, I'm not face down in bed." It can be exhausting.

So, when you see me staring at you at Starbucks, laughing with your friends, just know I'm a tad jealous. Cancer has robbed me of being carefree. I wonder if it will lessen over time.

As I have felt better, I have been fighting to win the happy memories of the ones I love. Here are the treasures I have stored in my heart. The moments in which I was able to be present.

Each moment seems special now. The truth is, that's the gift of cancer. The struggle is the fear. The fear of this amazing world of people marching forward without me in it. There is a lot of pride and arrogance in that thinking. A friend and I were talking about the control that comes with thinking life is as it should be with us in it. But the truth is, life is exactly planned. Our days are numbered. My job today is to live near to Jesus. To seek faithfulness. To have a peaceful heart that embraces each gift of joy as it comes. I long for the moments where I'm not screaming in my head and heart, "See me, I'm still alive! I'm right here!"

Connie Bader, Becky's good friend and teaching colleague, was planning an art trip for students during the coming summer. As a part of that process, she had an opportunity to visit locations in Europe ahead of time to check out some of the sites they might visit. She was allowed to take one person with her.

Normally, that person would be a spouse. However, Connie and her husband had other ideas. They both were excited to offer Becky the opportunity to travel with Connie, especially since one of the locations on the list was Barcelona, Spain! Connie knew Becky wanted to visit Spain someday, and she saw this as an opportunity to give her the gift of that experience.

From January 15-17, 2016, Becky and Connie took in as many sights and experiences as they could. They ate as much authentic Spanish food as they could. Becky said her paella was just as good as that which they ate in Spain! This pleased her as she had been making paella for her Spanish students for many years, claiming it was authentic! Apparently it was! Anyone who knows Becky and Connie would not be surprised to see them having fun imitating the sculpture in the background.

A couple months later, Becky and I took a trip to Destin, Florida, to visit her brother Dan and his wife Lisa. We also visited my parents who were living in Gainesville at the time. It was March, so we knew the weather could be questionable, but we expected to have some sunshine. By our last day in Destin, we had seen nothing but rain. Becky was determined to make the most of the time on the beachfront and decided we should get *some* beach time in, whether or not the weather cooperated. On our last day there, when it was obvious the weather was *not* going to cooperate, we put on our suits and went to the beach in the pouring rain, with lightning flashing out over the ocean. Lisa was our videographer, bravely documenting the moment when a lightning bolt struck as I was stepping into the breaking waves. We were making memories!

The opportunities to travel and have fun together while Becky was in remission were a great blessing. We didn't know how long it would last, but we were determined to make the most of each day!

One of Becky's favorite activities was spending time with her grandchildren. She loved reading to them, playing games with them, teaching

them, having tea parties with them and cooking with them. Whatever it took to have quality time together, she made it happen. She updated her cover photo shortly after one visit:

At the end of the school year in late May, she was celebrating with her students.

[May 23, 2016]

Celebrating the end of the school year with my students in Spanish 3. Best year ever!

At this point, Becky was telling me that every school year and every one of the classes she had the privilege to teach was the best ever. And I know she meant it. She loved teaching and she loved her students!

By the end of the summer, she was still feeling good. She was able to attend football games of her two favorite teams with her two favorite guys. She went to the Gopher game with her dad, and the Vikings game with me!

In December, our Christmas celebration was extra special, as our oldest daughter, Kristin, and her family had moved back within 90 minutes of us. Her husband Peter had accepted a call to serve two congregations in northeast

Iowa. Her posts reflected that appreciation for the opportunity to have our whole family together at that time.

[December 28, 2016]

First time together for Christmas since 2008. I love my family!

*C*hapter 9

Cancer – Part Two

This period of family joy and happiness ended up being a calm before the storm. In reality, by this time, Becky had been sensing that her cancer could be returning. Though neither her three-month checkup nor her CA-125 test results in October 2016 provided any hint that anything was changing, Becky was starting to notice the tell-tale signs of increasing abdominal discomfort and distention by the end of December. By the middle of January, Becky was starting to experience considerable discomfort. We knew what was happening before the tests were conducted on January 20, 2017. The PET scan showed extensive new cancer growth and her CA-125 numbers were over 1600, three times higher than during her initial diagnosis in 2014. The cancer was growing rapidly.

[January 24, 2017]

Dear Friends,

Following testing last week, it was confirmed yesterday that my cancer is back. I am sad. After a two-year cancer-free remission, Glenn and I were beginning to hope that maybe, just maybe, I was one of those women that would beat the statistical odds of ovarian cancer. Nope. It's not to be! My doctor's words from the August 12, 2014, initial diagnosis are ringing true: "Your cancer is inoperable and incurable, but treatable." So, we saddle up and get ready for the next phase of this journey. Because my cancer was very chemo-sensitive the first time around, my doctor is optimistic that a similar chemo regimen will be effective in shrinking the new tumors and possibly usher in a second cancer-free remission. The first of six chemo infusions, administered every four weeks, will be Thursday, Feb 2, 2017.

I was feeling emotionally drained last night after an evening of telephone calls and text messages to inform family and friends of the recurrent cancer. Right before heading to bed, I opened up a text message from my daughter, Karyn. Her spiritual words and insight buoyed my spirits:

"Dear Mama,

My heart aches thinking about you being in pain, being sick, having to go through chemo again. I'm so sorry this is happening. I'm so sorry you are suffering! Yet God is gracious. He has not allowed the cancer to spread out of control. He has given you skilled doctors to help guide you and dad through the process. He has given you family and friends who love you and will do anything to help you. And most of all, He has given you hope and peace through His Son's death on the cross. I do not know exactly what the future holds for you. This has been a terrifying thought the past few days. However, I do know that God is holding you in His almighty hands, and that He grants you and me, and all believers, forgiveness and salvation. "

She went on to quote **Psalm 73:23-26, Yet I am always with you; you hold me by my right hand. You guide me with your counsel, and afterward you will take me into glory. Whom have I in heaven but you? And earth has nothing I desire besides you. My flesh and my heart may fail, but God is the strength of my heart and my portion forever.**

I close with my go to passage from the past few weeks, **Philippians 4:6-7: Do not be anxious about anything, but in every situation, by prayer and petition, with thanksgiving, present your requests to God. And the peace of God, which transcends all understanding, will guard your hearts and your minds in Christ Jesus.** That peace which Paul speaks of is filling me up and keeping me going! I'm thankful for each one of you and covet your prayers on our behalf. To God be the glory!"

Becky's post didn't reflect the concern I had at that time. I knew how uncomfortable she was. We were both concerned that having to wait over a week to start the new chemo regimen could be a significant problem for her. I didn't understand why the doctors were waiting so long to get the treatments started. Fortunately, while she remained uncomfortable during that time due to the growing cancer, the pain and other symptoms didn't seem to get much worse. In the end, she was able to tolerate the discomfort and make it to her first chemo infusion without any major problems.

I also shared the news on my Facebook feed.

[January 24, 2017]

Dear Facebook friends, I know many of you have already seen this from Becky's page, but I wanted to share it as well. It is sad news but certainly not unexpected. It does bring a new reality to the lifestyle we've been able to enjoy, even though Becky has been living with cancer.

My emotions have been running just below the surface for a couple of days now, and as I type, I admit to a few tears. It's not just because of her situation but because of the unbelievable outpouring of love from our friends near and far. What a blessing it has been to have your support and your prayers to our faithful God who has already done everything we need. It is so powerful to read the passages of comfort you share from His Word. We are continually brought back to what is really important in our lives. Thank you all! Our trust is in Him. To God alone be the glory!

For Becky and me, the official diagnosis of the cancer returning was not a surprise. We were sure it had returned due to her symptoms and were ready for the next phase of the journey. Even so, it was still an emotional time, knowing that the many blessings we had experienced during the period of remission had come to an end. There would be more difficult times ahead.

Once again, the outpouring of love from so many meant a great deal to both of us. Not just love from our family and friends, but reminders of God's love for us as well. There is something special knowing that God is, indeed, our refuge and strength, and an ever-present help in trouble.

Becky and I had talked a little about retiring early during the previous year, knowing that was something we might want to do while Becky still felt good. When it became evident her cancer had returned, we started looking more seriously at that option. We made our decision together because we wanted to utilize our remaining time together as best we could.

On January 30, 2017, after prayerful consideration and with the knowledge that this cancer journey would likely be getting more difficult, Becky requested a peaceful release from her teaching call at Luther High School. In fact, we decided that both of us would retire early. It was a decision that God clearly blessed. The time we had together was wonderful, and the opportunity for me to be there for her, especially during the difficult days to come, was a great blessing!

In response to Becky's request, the Luther High School Board sent a wonderful letter to Becky on January 31, 2017:

> Dear Becky,
>
> Yesterday evening, the Luther High School Board of Control met for its regular monthly meeting. At this meeting, we read and considered your formal request to be peacefully released of your Divine Call as Spanish teacher at Luther High School. It was with heavy hearts that the Board of Control formally releases you effective at the end of this current school year.
>
> We sincerely appreciate your years of faithful service to the Lord as our Spanish teacher. Your passion and joy for teaching was always evident. You have touched the lives of many young Christians, and we give thanks to the Lord for your service. You will be in our constant prayers.
>
> May the following words that we considered last night for our opening devotion give you peace and encouragement: **2 Corinthians 4:17-18: For our light and momentary troubles are achieving for us an eternal glory that far outweighs them all. So we fix our eyes not on what is seen, but on what is unseen. For what is seen is temporary, but what is unseen is eternal.**

That beautiful passage from Corinthians really put things into perspective. The troubles we experience here on earth are momentary compared to the eternal glory we will experience in the future. That is what Becky fixed her eyes on, her future life in heaven.

In the meantime, we were still here and needed to deal with the realities of cancer. Becky had her first infusion on February 2, 2017.

[February 4, 2017]

Dear Friends,

The phrase "The Lord will provide" has been running through my mind since the recent news that my cancer has returned. The middle-of-the-night anxieties roll over me. Shhh...the Lord will provide. Worries about how the future will unfold weigh me down. Shhh...the Lord will provide.

These worries and anxieties have been of a temporal nature, and in many cases I have seen directly how the Lord is providing. My oncologist retired at the end of December. The Lord has provided me with a wonderful new doctor. My students have Chromebooks and access to Google Classroom so I am able to set up online learning activities for them while I am absent from school. Glenn and I have the financial stability to be able to retire at the end of this school year. The list goes on.

Yesterday I read through Genesis 22:1-14, the account of Abraham being asked to sacrifice his son, Isaac, and the portion of Scripture from where I remember the phrase "The Lord will provide." What a powerful reminder to me that way beyond providing for my temporal needs, God has provided for my eternal future. At one point in the story, Isaac speaks up and says to his father Abraham, "Father?" "Yes, my son?" Abraham replies. "The fire and wood are here," Isaac says, "but where is the lamb for the burnt offering?" Abraham answers, "God himself will provide the lamb for the burnt offering, my son."

And God did provide. He provided a ram in a nearby thicket to be sacrificed in place of Isaac. Abraham called that place "The Lord Will Provide." Years later on that very same mountain God did not spare his own Son, but gave Him up for us all. Jesus suffered the ultimate sacrifice in our place so that our sins would be forgiven. We now have a home waiting for us in heaven. **Romans 8:37: In all these**

things we are more than conquerors through Him who loved us!
The Lord has indeed provided!

My first of six chemo infusions was Thursday. Side effects have been manageable. There have been some similarities and some differences from my first chemo experience. A few more days should give me a realistic picture of what I can expect following subsequent treatments. Glenn is at my side as we journey down this path again. We are so thankful for your continued prayers and encouragement!

I will close with a note I received from my Dad last night:

"Just a little email note to let you know that Mom and I are thinking of you today. We hope and pray that the chemo treatments you are again undergoing will bear the same fruit that they did when your cancer was first discovered. We do such praying because of what James tells us in the 4th chapter of his epistle: **'You do not have, because you do not ask God!'** So, we lay our pleas before God, telling Him what we would like to see done in your situation, and then we leave it up to Him. If He answers our prayers in a different way than what we request, we accept that also, knowing that **'As the heavens are higher than the earth, so are my ways higher than your ways, and my thoughts than your thoughts.' Isaiah 55:9.** God bless you, dear daughter!"

I love you, dear Dad!

When Becky put together her Facebook posts, she wrote drafts first. She had themes she wanted to highlight and Scripture she wanted to use. She usually used up all or most of her material in what she posted. However, in this case, she left out a lot. She had numerous thoughts on the topic "The Lord will provide" that she did not include.

Following are her additional personal notes on "The Lord Will Provide" from February 3, 2017. These paragraphs provide a deeper insight into the emotional challenges she was feeling as she waited for her first chemo treatment and as we considered early retirement.

"The Lord will provide" comforts me when worries fill my mind during the dark hours of a sleepless night. The ten days between the official diagnosis and the start of chemo were tough. I continued to teach, a huge blessing in terms of filling my day with purpose and wonderful people. I felt pretty good from the neck up, but the discomfort caused by cancer was evident in abdominal bloating and pain. I pushed through each day, sometimes feeling like I was having an out-of-body experience. My clear head would get in the groove of teaching, and then the bell would ring and I would lose that groove and feel the discomfort and be reminded, "Oh, yeah, I have cancer!"

Both Glenn and I wondered if the cancer would take over before the chemo infusions began. I wonder how long I have to live. These are not thoughts of despair, but more of contemplating what dying will be like and wondering how wonderful heaven will be. I have no reference point for something perfectly wonderful. I keep hanging on the promise that the Lord will provide.

"The Lord will provide" helps us plan for the future. Glenn and I are at that age when retirement is part of the conversation. I will turn 58 in April. Our plan was that I would teach three more years and retire at age 61, at which time Glenn would retire at age 62. After much discussion and prayerful consideration, we have decided to retire sooner. I'll retire at the end of the school year and Glenn will follow sometime this spring or summer. It was a bittersweet decision for me. I love what I do, but at the same time I am at peace with the decision. I had no plans to be a high school Spanish teacher, but God did and He put me in this position 22 years ago. Similarly, now, I had no plans to retire this year, but it's obvious to me that through cancer, God is leading me in this direction. Isn't it wonderful that God's plans are perfect! The Lord will provide.

"The Lord will provide" comes in the form of support from my family, friends, acquaintances and even people I have never met. Glenn is my rock. How could he know on the day of our wedding that he would be living out the vows, "for better or for worse, in sickness and in health, 'til death us do part." God is giving him what he needs to provide me with spiritual, emotional and physical support.

How gracious God has been to me, too, in plopping Mike and Karyn in La Crosse two years ago, and Pete and Kristin just 90 minutes away in northeast Iowa just one year ago. I am so grateful I can spend time with my children and grandchildren on a regular basis. There's also the unbelievable outpouring of support from friends, acquaintances and perfect strangers. The Lord has provided me with an army of prayer warriors who storm heaven's gate on my behalf. Thank you!

For the second set of chemo infusions, the doctors modified the medications, changing out the Taxol for Doxil. Doxil is tinted red, and is not so affectionately known as "the red devil." The good news was that Taxol was the drug that caused hair loss, so for this round, she would keep her hair!

The bad news was that Doxil generally was harder on the body. As Becky noted, the prior post was written just before the effects of the chemo really hit. Her next post provided a better perspective of how she felt when they did.

[February 7, 2017]

Dear Friends,

I turned a chemo corner last night. Unlike my first bout with cancer and subsequent chemo treatments two years ago, nausea has been my nemesis this time around. My first response was to try and tough it out. When that didn't work, I took the prescribed drugs. The drugs didn't put a dent in the nausea. Yesterday, I contacted my provider and she prescribed two new drugs. Within minutes of taking them, I started to feel some relief. What a wonderful feeling!

This cancer/chemo journey is fraught with such emotional ups and downs. I feel up when I physically feel well; I feel down when my body is experiencing pain and discomfort. I don't like being on this cancer journey again. I don't like feeling crummy. I don't like feeling unproductive.

There are a lot of things I don't like about this, but this is my journey, whether I like it or not! The Lord brings me back from my complaining when He speaks to me through **Isaiah 43: But now, this is what the Lord says — he who created you, Jacob, he who formed you, Israel: "Do not fear, for I have redeemed you; I have summoned you by name; you are mine. When you pass through the waters, I will be with you; and when you pass through the rivers, they will not sweep over you. When you walk through the fire, you will not be burned; the flames will not set you ablaze. For I am the Lord your God, the Holy One of Israel, your Savior."** I am His! Thank you, friends, for your continued prayers. To God be the glory!

February 4th through 6th were difficult days. But once she got past those days, she felt so much better. She was eager to return to school.

[February 8, 2017]

Dear Friends,

It was so good to be back at school today! I couldn't exactly put my finger on why it felt so right, but a friend put into words what I was feeling. She said, "You are now on the journey." She was right. For several weeks, I suspected the cancer was back so the unknown caused anxiety. Once it was diagnosed, I was anxious because it really was back! And then there was the anxiety of chemo and how I would respond. Well, now all those things are behind me. Yes, the cancer is back, and the chemo side effects were awful, but I got through it. I know where things stand now. I'm on the cancer journey again and it's going to be okay. Each day is a gift of God's grace. **Psalm 118:24: This is the day the Lord has made; let us rejoice and be glad in it.**

[February 9, 2017]

DO NOT BE AFRAID - an anthem by Philip Stopford

Today I received a gift unlike any gift I have ever received. During my sixth-hour prep time, the Luther High Sound Foundation came into my classroom. They invited me to sit in one of the desks. Then they formed a circle around me and started to sing. I bowed my head, closed my eyes, and wept as the beautiful message of the Gospel washed over me in glorious sound.

Isaiah 43:1-2: Do not be afraid, for I have redeemed you, I have called you by name, you are mine.

It's one thing to hear God's Words being read, but it's another to hear them put to music and to let them wash over you in glorious sound! Becky made a side note to her family: I would like this sung at my funeral by current and/or former Sound Foundation members. The song was not only sung beautifully for her at her funeral but it was also sung for her twice more in the weeks before she died.

Becky loved spending time with her children and grandchildren. Her mother-daughter relationships were special to her. When we were parents of young children living far away from our families in Salt Lake City, UT, and

Norman, OK, Becky longed for occasional relief from her child-raising responsibilities. She often wished her mother was close by to not only dote on our children, but to give her a break as well. It was from those experiences that she was determined to provide as much help for her daughters as she could, knowing how much that help would mean to them in those challenging child-rearing years. She loved to be the support system for both of our daughters, however they needed it.

[February 24, 2017]

Girls' night out with these lovely ladies to celebrate Karyn's 30th birthday. I am so blessed to call my daughters friends!

Becky designed and sewed costumes for drama productions at Luther High School for 20 years. She and Connie made quite a team, as both were talented artists. The students followed their lead by creating some truly memorable shows.

The spring show of 2017 was the last show for which Becky would take on these responsibilities. She had a little more help that year due to her cancer and the more challenging chemo treatments. Still, she put in a lot of time! With the excellent assistance she received, she was able to complete the work with wonderful results!

[March 9, 2017]

In 2002, Connie Bader and I collaborated on our first musical, Rodgers and Hammerstein's *Oklahoma!* Daughter Kristin Faugstad played the role of Laurie. Due to my retirement at the end this school year, this year's musical/operetta, *Pirates of Penzance,* will be the last official Bader/Lussky collaboration. How cool that, once again, daughter Kristin is part of the team, this time in the role of vocal coach and director. It's been a blast working together with Kristin on this show!

Following the final performance on March 12, 2017, Becky was invited to say a few words. She knew she would have that opportunity and wanted to make sure she appropriately reflected how she felt, so she had written out ahead of time what she wanted to say:

Seventeen years ago, Connie and I embarked on our crazy drama adventure. Our first show was Thornton Wilder's, "The Matchmaker." The following year we produced our first musical, "Oklahoma!" Since then, we have collaborated on seven more dramas and eight more musicals, not to mention countless children's theater productions. While it's true that our drama productions have been a team effort, every team needs a leader. Year after year, I have been blown away by the artistic vision and creativity that Connie brings to each production as our director. This year was no exception. Please join me in thanking my dear friend for her efforts and acknowledge the gifts with which God has blessed her.

*Connie and I planned to retire together in several years. However, my cancer recurrence has changed those plans. Today's performance is my last official show as a member of Luther's drama team. It's bittersweet to say the least. And yet, it's also a testament to God's grace. With the cancer's return, I did not feel well back in January and I wondered, "How in the world am I going to fulfill my obligations as a teacher and a costumer?" St. Paul, in Philippians chapter 4 reminded me, **Do not be anxious about anything.** In other words, God was saying to me "I've got this. The cancer may be back, but you still have work to do." So here I am! He provided me with a wonderful sewing team, help with program creation and a new home for the cast party. Thank you for all the help!*

Cast, you know I love every one of you as my own kids. You lift me up just by being you! And to all of you here, thank you for your continued prayers on my behalf.

Sir Arthur Sullivan wrote the music for "Pirates of Penzance," but he is also the composer of many well-known hymn tunes. One of my favorites of his is, "I'm But a Stranger Here, Heaven is My Home." This hymn speaks to my situation. I am back on a chemo regimen which is again showing favorable results. My doctor is optimistic that I am a good candidate for another remission. It appears I have more living to do! I am thankful for the gift of time. However, none of us must forget that our home here on earth is temporary. Jesus has secured an eternal home for us in heaven through his perfect life, innocent death, and resurrection from the grave. Heaven is our home! Thanks be to God who gives us the victory through our Lord Jesus Christ. To God be the glory!

I think there were a lot of tears in the audience and on the stage that evening as everyone rose to give her a standing ovation.

Drama season was always one of great drama, and I mean that in every possible way. Becky had very little time to do much else during her free time from January through the last performance in March, except work on her drama responsibilities. Every year, it was a stressful period for us, as I'm sure the same holds true for the other coaches during their seasons. In Becky's case, she worked on costumes every night until at least 9 p.m. and at least 12 hours a day on weekends. We did try to set aside an hour late each evening to connect while watching a TV show, which was her time to wind down before retiring each evening.

Along with the stress, however, came immense joy. Joy when it was all over but also joy because of the incredible connections she was able to make with her drama students. Becky always said drama season was like going through childbirth. It was painful as long as it lasted, but the results were so wonderful you decided it was all worth it. When Becky said this last performance for her was bittersweet, I understood exactly how she was feeling. Considerable relief that all the work was behind her, but sadness that this wonderful part of her life was now over.

[March 29, 2017]

Dear Friends,

Today was my third chemo infusion. This marks the halfway point – YAY! After my fourth infusion at the end of April, I will have a CT scan which will show definitively if the chemo is knocking back the cancer. In the meantime, I have strong indications that the chemo is indeed working to shrink the tumors. The cancer pain that I experienced prior to starting chemo is gone! The CA125 ovarian cancer marker has plummeted dramatically. After my first infusion it dropped from 1690 to 213. Normal is under 35. I am very thankful that not only does it appear the chemo is working, but because of that, I feel well, with plenty of energy to live a normal life with my family and my students! Thank you for praying for me! It appears that God is answering those prayers with, "I still have plans for you." I look forward to the new doors that He is going to open for me in retirement!

Physically, I feel well. I have to admit, however, that I struggle emotionally. Dealing with this cancer recurrence has been much more difficult than coping with the initial diagnosis two and half years ago. Hearing my doctor say, "I am sorry to have to tell you that you have stage 4 ovarian cancer" was a shock to say the least. But within two months, after just three treatments, my CA125 level was in the normal range and a PET/CT scan showed no tumors! "Very unusual," were the words of my doctor. I became hopeful during my two-year remission that the cancer would not return.

This recurrence is a reminder that my cancer isn't going to go away. Sometimes it makes me sad. Sometimes I wake up in the middle of the night with the thought, "I don't want to have cancer again!" I cry easily at random times, having to fight back tears when I want the moment to be private but I am in public. And so, I find myself straddling two worlds. I am not afraid to die. I look forward to living with Jesus forever in heaven. Heaven is my home!

But in the meantime, I am living here on earth and I like that, too! How do I balance the two? I think the Apostle Paul had similar feelings because he wrote these words in **Philippians 1:21-26, For to me, to live is Christ and to die is gain. If I am to go on living in the body, this will mean fruitful labor for me. Yet what shall I choose? I do not know! I am torn between the two: I desire to depart and be with Christ, which is better by far; but it is more necessary for you that I remain in the body. Convinced of this, I know that I will remain, and I will continue with all of you for your progress and joy in the faith, so that through my being with you again your boasting in Christ Jesus will abound on account of me.**

Lent is such a wonderful time to take the focus off of me and put it on my Savior Jesus who willingly suffered an agonizing death on the cross to pay for my sins. In my morning devotion from a few days ago, the author wrote, "There is peace, hope and joy in Christ crucified. We can live joyfully through each day, knowing that our God will sustain us. We can sleep in safety each night under the shadow of His wings." How thankful I am that we are redeemed, restored, forgiven. To God be the glory!

We were thrilled the chemo was working so well once again. However, this second round of chemo was physically more difficult for Becky. Additionally, I don't think either of us were expecting the emotional struggle she would have the second time around. The realization that the cancer would almost certainly continue to return was hard for her, especially as she was going through the chemo-related nausea every few weeks. Knowing that these treatments would not eliminate the cancer, even though they were temporarily effective, Becky thought a lot about how she wanted to live her remaining days on earth, and that was an emotional struggle for her.

*C*hapter 10
Remission – Part Two

The following month, Becky started researching alternatives to chemo, including natural and holistic remedies. Our daughters, who had been following some of those nutritional regimens for a number of years, were able to provide insights as well. Once again, Becky was intellectually stimulated by the knowledge she was gaining.

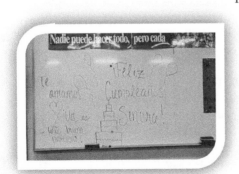

Meanwhile, she cherished time with her family and students. Becky loved the family time with Kristin's family over Easter, and her students helped her celebrate her 58th birthday in late April.

[April 27, 2017]

Thank you for thinking of me on my birthday. Along with your well-wishes, my students and family made sure I felt extra-special on my 58th birthday.

The culmination of all of Becky's research and prayer was reflected in her post shortly thereafter.

[April 30, 2017]

Dear Friends,

I have come to a crossroads in my cancer journey. My recurrence in January made me realize that while chemo knocked my cancer back for two years, it wasn't going to keep it away forever. Chemo treats the symptoms of cancer but doesn't get at the underlying cause. After three of the recommended six infusions here is where I'm at: my cancer symptoms are gone (abdominal bloating and pelvic pain); my cancer number (CA125) is in the normal range (17, down from 1690 in January); and the CT scan shows that the chemo has reduced the size of the tumors but not completely eliminated them. I thank God for these blessings. However, chemo was messing with me physically, and more importantly, emotionally. I started reading about alternative ways to treat cancer and after prayerful consideration I have decided to discontinue chemo in favor of healing my body through a holistic approach.

I know that chemo can shrink the tumors, but it will never cure my cancer. I am curious to see if my body's immune system can heal naturally if I treat it well through natural means: diet, exercise, stress elimination, etc. If I don't try this, I will never know! So, I need to try it! While this is not my doctor's Plan A (more chemo) or Plan B (more chemo and surgery), I appreciated that she listened to me and is respectful of my decision. She calls it Plan C. More importantly,

Glenn is supportive of my decision as we angle off together on a new leg of this cancer journey.

I have a three-month follow-up CT scan and doctor appointment scheduled for July. In the meantime, I am excited to move forward with my decision to work toward natural healing through nourishing my body. I met with a nutritionist two weeks ago and she set me up with dietary supplements to boost my immune system, detoxify my liver, aid digestion and promote cellular healing. At the same time I have eliminated refined sugar, processed foods and dairy from my diet.

What's left, you ask? Among other things, delicious fresh fruits and vegetables, eggs, nuts, legumes (I love garbanzo beans), fish, coconut milk, and lots of herbs and spices to spice things up! I honestly really enjoy eating this way! Ultimately, this isn't about me at all, but the perfect plan that God has laid out in advance for my life here on earth. I have prayed for His guidance and I now ask that He bless my decision.

Psalm 139:13-17: For you created my inmost being; you knit me together in my mother's womb. I praise you because I am fearfully and wonderfully made; your works are wonderful, I know that full well. My frame was not hidden from you when I was made in the secret place, when I was woven together in the depths of the earth. Your eyes saw my unformed body; all the days ordained for me were written in your book before one of them came to be. How precious to me are your thoughts, God! How vast is the sum of them!

Your continued prayers and encouragement are greatly appreciated!

Becky fully embraced this new lifestyle. She spent a lot of time preparing healthy foods that she really enjoyed. She dutifully used the supplements recommended by her nutritionist, and she continued to exercise regularly. With this new lifestyle, she lost weight, kept her muscles toned, and felt good overall. I still enjoyed some of the foods she no longer ate, but I also learned to appreciate some of the recipes she was using. Fortunately, Becky loved them and was able to consistently adhere to her new diet!

We didn't know if Becky's new anti-cancer diet would keep the disease at bay, but we learned that she felt better than she did while enduring chemo treatments. This was largely a quality of life decision that we both embraced for her. Still, we trusted that God's will would be done no matter what health path we took.

As Becky moved into this new phase of life, she wanted to live each day to the fullest. When Luther High School hosted a donkey basketball game in early May, Becky was determined to participate. She didn't play the first half, when the donkeys were rather agitated and nasty. By the time Becky went in, they had settled down a bit and she was proudly able to get onto her donkey.

She also was reveling in the last weeks of her teaching career. Finally, on her last day of school, her final class arrived.

[May 19, 2017]

My last official class as Señora, 7th-hour Spanish 1.

It's a surreal feeling that this chapter of my life has ended. How blessed I have been at Luther for the past 22 years! Thank you, Lord, for the privilege of teaching these wonderful young people!

A few days later, Connie and the students gave Becky a wonderful send-off. Following are excerpts from a tribute to Becky that Connie wrote for her final farewell with the student body:

> Becky came to Luther to fill the Spanish position in the summer of 1995. Her kind and cheerful demeanor drew us close to her immediately. She was always a team player. She took time to relate to her students and they returned her love. They called her Señora. The students loved her classes. Passing by her room on any given day, she'd be cooking, singing, acting and worshiping, all in Spanish, of course.
>
> She's been more than a teacher. She's a "Top Notch Teacher", nominated by her students. It was never unusual to see students just hanging out in her classroom. She's compassionate and caring. She counsels and comforts with God's promises. She knows what it's like to go through fiery trials. She's fought the ugly cancer cells three times now! She understands the challenges God puts in our lives and how all things work for good to those who love him! Even though Becky is retiring from teaching, she will not retire from living her days to the fullest to give honor and glory to the Lord who has been her faithful guide.
>
> The drama team never got the chance to transition our skills to the new auditorium this year. But the cast of *Pirates of Penzance* has a farewell song based on one from the show. I'm sure these words speak the sentiments felt by the student body, faculty and members of the association.

> Señora, dear - we honor thee
> For years of dedication
> In teaching, advising, guiding us
> For future occupations
> Don't take our lack of words
> As truth of our emotion
>
> You are to us as sweet a rhyme
> As a Gilbert and Sullivan Poem
> Hail, Señora, thou Heav'n-born maid!
> Thou Fairest of the teacher's trade!
> Hail, flowing fount of sentiment.
> All hail, all hail, divine emollient!

For those not familiar, that was a takeoff on one of the songs from *Pirates of Penzance*. What a great gift from a wonderful colleague and special group of students!

Becky's official retirement date was June 30, 2017, though she was finished with her school year duties by the end of May. She got her room and teaching materials ready for the upcoming Spanish teacher during June, but otherwise was ready to start living her retirement life.

Since I also retired at the end of June, we dove head first into our new life together. We spent a week up north at the lake, just the two of us. Becky loved sitting on the dock reading her books, going for boat rides, taking the paddleboard out early in the morning from one end of the lake to the other. At the lake, it was quiet and peaceful, away from the everyday bustle at home.

We also spent a lot of time with our children and their families. Life was good!

[July 21, 2017]

Dear Friends,

Back in April, I decided to discontinue chemo treatments in favor of a holistic approach to healing my body from cancer. My doctor recommended a follow-up exam in July to evaluate things. Today was the day! What would the CT scan reveal? Rejoice with me that God has graciously granted me another remission. He has answered the prayers of many with the gift of renewed health. Once again, I am humbled by this gift of time.

Psalm 103: Praise the LORD, my soul; all my inmost being, praise his holy name. Praise the LORD, my soul, and forget not all his benefits—who forgives all your sins and heals all your diseases, who redeems your life from the pit and crowns you with love and compassion, who satisfies your desires with good things so that your youth is renewed like the eagle's.

I love my new way of life. A host of interesting recipes makes for great-tasting food and it's virtually impossible to overeat. It's so freeing to no longer struggle with food addictions. I have done some modifications in the realm of personal hygiene as well – no more shampoo or deodorant. I've started using coconut oil as toothpaste, make-up remover and moisturizer. A person can really go crazy trying to avoid environmental toxins in foods and household products. I'm trying to find a balance.

Why make these changes in my life? Dr. David Servan-Schreiber wrote the book *Anti-Cancer, A New Way of Life*. His ideas resonated with me. I am following to some degree or other these suggestions to change my body's terrain:

1. **Clean up the diet**. I am reducing/eliminating sugar which feeds cancer growth and inflammation. I am also reducing/eliminating pro-inflammatory omega-6 fatty acids including red meats, dairy, corn, sunflower, soybean and safflower oils, and trans fats.

2. **Add anti-cancer foods.** I have added to our diet foods that help fight cancer, such as anticancer herbs and spices (green tea, turmeric, ginger, thyme, rosemary, mint, basil, sage), omega-3 rich foods (salmon, sardines, mackerel, walnuts, green vegetables), cruciferous vegetables (broccoli, cauliflower,

cabbage), garlic, onions and leeks, red berries, plums, blueberries, dark chocolate (more than 70 percent cocoa), and even a little bit of red wine.

3. **Engage in physical activity.** I don't have to run marathons, or even run at all. I walk rapidly for 30 minutes a day, six times a week.

4. **Manage responses to stress.** We can't avoid all stress in our lives, but we can learn to respond differently.

5. **Clean up the immediate environment.** We got rid of all indoor pollutants, parabens and phthalates in cosmetics, and scratched Teflon pans.

It's an interesting journey. A friend of mine wrote, "I do believe all things are in the Lord's hands, but He has given us a choice to use His things for our blessing." I agree. I always pray that God will guide and direct the decisions I make concerning my physical health. I am thankful that my spiritual health is taken care of through Jesus!

I should probably comment on Becky's note that she no longer used deodorant. That sounds like it might have been a potential social problem, but I assure you it wasn't. She stopped using deodorant, but she replaced the deodorant with coconut oil which we found was also effective for that purpose. A part of Becky's research during the preceding months led her to use coconut oil for many unique things besides deodorant, including skin and hair conditioner.

Knowing there was a good chance Becky's cancer would come back in the next year, Becky had a bucket list item to take a trip out east to see friends and family. We also had a trip planned to San Diego and Santa Barbara, CA, in September. So, in the fall of 2017, we had a number of wonderful opportunities to travel.

[September 16, 2017]

We had a wonderful visit with Glenn's folks and sister, Marilyn, in San Diego. We spent an afternoon at Fleet Science Center and the Botanical Gardens in Balboa Park. What an impressive and beautiful place!

Shortly after we returned from our California trip, we celebrated our 34th wedding anniversary. This was our fourth anniversary celebration after Becky's original diagnosis with ovarian cancer. We were so thankful for each of these bonus years.

[September 24, 2017]

Celebrating our 34th wedding anniversary as we say farewell to summer at the lake. Our wedding text says it well, **Oh give thanks unto the Lord, for He is good, for His mercy endures forever.**

I wrote:

[September 24, 2017]

Pretty lucky guy to have married this wonderful lady 34 years ago today! She told me a few years ago we were living our bonus years once our children had moved out of the house. She didn't realize two of them would move back in for a short time, but she still got it right. We're enjoying these bonus years and thankful for each one God gives us!

While we were enjoying our retirement as a couple very much, Becky also wanted to spend as much time as she could with her family, including her seven grandchildren. It didn't take much coaxing on the part of her daughters to make that happen.

[September 25, 2017]

WHEN THE LORD CLOSES A DOOR, SOMEWHERE HE OPENS A WINDOW

Retirement from teaching came a few years earlier than expected due to a cancer recurrence in January. To quote the Reverend Mother from my favorite movie, *The Sound of Music*, "When the Lord closes a door somewhere He opens a window." The window that God opened for me is the opportunity to teach three of our grandchildren: Marit and Greta Faugstad (ages 9 and 7) and Isaac Lukasek (age 6).

Our daughters are both homeschool moms. Kristin was the first to broach the subject of me teaching piano to Marit and Greta. The irony is that Kristin is herself an accomplished pianist and former piano teacher. To my credit, however, Kristin did spend her first two years of piano instruction under my tutelage and she turned out okay. I didn't have to think too long before agreeing to Kristin's request. When Karyn jumped on board the piano train with Isaac, she asked if I would also teach art to Isaac. She said she would provide the curriculum. More irony, since Karyn is the family artist and illustrator. Sure! Why not be an art teacher, too!

So, how's this for irony? I'm teaching piano to the children of my daughter, Kristin, the pianist. I'm teaching art to the son of my daughter, Karyn, the artist. Under the circumstances, it seemed fitting that I should be teaching Spanish too, since that's my specialty! So, I am! On Wednesdays, I spend the morning with Abel (age 2) while Karyn, Isaac and Matthias (age 4) participate in activities sponsored by the La Crosse Area Homeschool Co-op. After lunch, Isaac comes home with me for his piano, Spanish and art lessons. On Thursdays, I make the 90-minute drive to Iowa where the Faugstads live. I teach piano, Spanish and art to Marit and Greta. Younger brothers James (age 5) and Nels (age 16 months) get some grandma time too.

It was bittersweet to walk away from teaching this past May, but how thankful I am that God has extended my teaching career when He opened this special window for me with my grandchildren.

I have to admit when I first heard the girls talking to Becky about this, I was kind of dumbfounded. Why would a college piano performance major not want to teach her own children piano herself? And why would a college studio art major not want to teach her own child art? However, the opportunity to have scheduled time every week with her children and grandchildren was a perfect fit for what Becky wanted in her retirement. The fact that she could continue in her role as a teacher was icing on the cake.

In the coming year, these weekly teaching dates and grandma time were the highlights of Becky's life. She cherished these opportunities, and I'm positive our grandchildren loved their time with her as well. Becky, as she had always done for her classes at Luther, spent time preparing for school days to make sure the subjects were taught well and that her grandkids were having fun. In addition, Becky's efforts helped our daughters considerably. This new year of teaching benefitted everybody!

[October 16, 2017]

This summer I found these seven little cuties at the ReStore in Spooner, WI. I bought one each for Marit, Greta, Isaac, James, Matthias, Nels and Abel.

It turns out the collection is already growing. Kristin Faugstad and Karyn Lukasek are not only expecting but are due two

weeks apart in late March and early April! Such happy news for our family!

This was Becky's announcement to our Facebook family that both our daughters were expecting. We were all excited to have two new babies join the family in another five to six months!

In October, we took off on our trip to the East Coast. After stopping at Niagara Falls and visiting friends in upstate New York, we continued east and spent a few days on the rocky shores of Maine. From there we travelled to see family from both sides of the family in Massachusetts, New Jersey and Ohio. It was an extra special trip to see her cousins in New Jersey, as Becky hadn't been out there since she was a young girl. She also knew this was most likely the last time she would spend time with those cousins.

[October 21, 2017]

When we made the decision to retire earlier this year, I casually mentioned to Glenn hat I would like to take a road trip to visit my cousins in New Jersey. Glenn Lussky, master trip-planner and husband extraordinaire, turned that wish into a reality with a 10-day, 3,200 mile road trip through 15 states and one Canadian province. Along the way we saw spectacular sites and visited dear friends and relatives. I kept the atlas close at hand, learning things about the geography of our country that I probably should have already known! Google searches on my phone allowed us to find out-of-the-way places as well as information about the history of New England and the Mid-Atlantic states.

I wondered how ten days on the road would work with my modified diet. No problem! I made food ahead of time which we stored in an electric cooler with a car-plug-in. In addition to that, our hosts were so kind to prepare food that I could eat. Thank you!

We enjoyed each leg of our journey and will cherish the memories for years to come!

One of the challenges of Becky's diet was the need for her to make food that adhered to her strict anti-cancer diet. Whenever we traveled, Becky had to prepare enough food to eat during our trips. Each time we went to the lake, we brought at least one cooler filled with fresh vegetables and prepared foods. We had two coolers for this East Coast trip, which was just enough!

By this time we were four months into our retirement. We had spent time at the lake and taken two trips which took us from California to Maine. It was time to start settling into our fall and winter routines, which included a three-month check-up with Becky's oncologist.

[October 31, 2017]

Dear Friends,

Today was my three-month cancer follow-up. My CA-125 number was seven, well within the normal range. I have no physical symptoms and the doctor's exam showed no abnormalities. Wow! God continues to bless me with the gift of good health. It's fitting on this day, which happens to mark the 500th anniversary of the Lutheran Reformation, to praise and thank our gracious God with the words from the Psalms on which Martin Luther based his *hymn A Mighty Fortress Is Our God.* **Psalm 46:1: God is my refuge and strength, an ever-present help in trouble.** It's fitting also because a little more than three years ago God used these very same words to calm my anxious spirit.

How thankful I am that 500 years ago God used his servant, Martin Luther, to proclaim the truth that we are saved through faith alone in Jesus. Today God continues to strengthen and sustain me in my faith through His Word and Sacraments!

[November 10, 2017]

Dear Friends,

This weekend the La Crosse area will be filled with music flowing from the 50th anniversary celebration of the WELS Choral Festival. It's been fun thinking back on my choral fest experience with the Lakeside Acapella group when we traveled to Mobridge, SD, during my senior year in high school. I have one vivid memory of Mr. Dave Adickes and the Luther High School Sound Foundation. I had never seen a director as full of energy as Mr. Adickes, and I had never heard a choir accompanied by canned music before. Sound Foundation was cutting edge in the fall of 1976. I never dreamed at the time that one day I would be a teaching colleague of Mr. Adickes at Luther and that both our daughters would sing in Sound Foundation! I can't wait until the Sunday concert when I will join together with 500 high school singers and 300 alumni singers in the closing number, *God's Word Is Our Great Heritage.* What a blessing music has been in my life.

Notice the young lady in the front row, third from the left in the picture below? That was Becky singing in the Lakeside High School Acapella Choir in the fall of 1976!

Our friend, Andy, passed away on November 16, 2017, due to complications from sarcoma. He was 48 years old, had lived less than two years after his cancer diagnosis, and had many challenges with his treatments during that time. We were privileged to be friends with Andy and his family during our respective cancer journeys and appreciated the opportunity to visit Andy before he died. We were living through many of the same challenges, but they experienced the sadness of Andy's departure from their lives first.

Becky wrote Andy's family a letter after he died, a portion of which is noted below:

We will continue to pray for you as you mourn the loss of your husband and father. May God strengthen and carry you through the days of grief and turn them once again to days filled with joy and laughter.

We knew that day was coming for us as well. We were thankful for all our friends and family who were praying similar prayers for us.

Chapter 11

Cancer – Part Three

[January 8, 2018]

Dear Friends,

The old year now has passed away, and what a memorable year 2017 was! A cancer recurrence in January put into motion our plans for retirement. A nine-month cancer remission allowed for lake time, travel, house projects and my favorite activity, teaching three of our grandchildren piano, art and Spanish. We rejoiced at the announcement that both the Faugstad and Lukasek families would be welcoming new babies in 2018. Multiple gatherings with family and friends during the Christmas holidays brought a year filled with earthly blessings to a close.

Another new year is upon us, and 2018 is starting off in the same way as 2017, with another recurrence of cancer. A CT scan last Thursday revealed that my cancer has returned, this time in the form of a 12 cm tumor in my pelvis. I will have surgery this coming Friday to remove the mass. We will determine a follow-up treatment plan after surgery. My doctor is optimistic that this new cancer is treatable. She is confident that I will be around to hold my new grandchildren this spring. I would like that!

Last April I made some major lifestyle changes. I was very curious to see whether or not adopting an anti-cancer diet would strengthen my immune system to the point that my body's terrain would not support another cancer invasion. It's apparent that this didn't happen. However, God richly blessed me in many ways through this lifestyle change! I am free from cravings, the food I prepare is delicious, I sleep well, my energy level is high, and maintaining my weight is a breeze. I am so thankful for these unexpected blessings!

Living with cancer is a roller-coaster ride. During a remission, I become hopeful that I will be one of the statistical anomalies that is cured from stage 4 ovarian cancer. A recurrence quickly brings me back to the reality that this most likely won't be the case. Sadness and fear set in – sadness that I won't be around to serve my family and fear of the pain and ugliness of the dying process. Cancer is a sobering reminder that we live in a world tainted by sin. Our bodies break down from disease and aging. Ultimately, we die.

Honestly, though, as God's redeemed child, sadness and fear are completely overshadowed by hope and peace – hope that is built on nothing less than Jesus' blood and righteousness and peace that transcends all understanding and guards my heart and mind in Christ Jesus. The anxieties that so easily arise are calmed time and time again by the promises found in the Gospel. My sins are forgiven through faith in Jesus. I have peace with God. Heaven is my home.

Living with cancer has become the new normal for me and Glenn. We thank God for the time of grace He has provided. We treasure times of remission. Please continue to keep us in your prayers as we navigate this cancer journey, fully confident that in all things God works for the good of those who love him, who have been called according to his purpose.

Romans 8:38-39: For I am convinced that neither death nor life, neither angels nor demons, neither the present nor the future, nor any powers, neither height nor depth, nor anything else in all creation, will be able to separate us from the love of God that is in Christ Jesus our Lord.

This was the first time Becky's cancer was deemed treatable with surgery. In the previous two occurrences, the cancer was located throughout her lymph system and her abdomen. This time, the doctors felt they could get at the cancer through a surgical process. This tumor was much larger than the previous two, but they didn't see anything on the PET scans that indicated surgery would be a problem. They also took the opportunity at this time to perform a complete hysterectomy, hoping that maybe the removal of her ovaries might slow down the development of new tumors.

This was a significant surgery. Aside from the hysterectomy, they removed a very large tumor and scraped cancer growths from much of her abdominal cavity. The doctor indicated to me after the surgery that it was a best case result. Despite this positive report, we knew the doctors could only remove the cancer cells they could visibly see and that were accessible. We knew many cancer cells would remain in her body, and they would continue to grow and spread. We knew there was still work to do to try to combat the cancer, even after the surgery.

It was amazing to me that only six hours after surgery, Becky's doctors and nurses had her standing and walking in an effort to prevent blood clots from forming. Kris, a friend of ours who was a nurse, stopped by for an hour that evening to help Becky. Becky had no recollection of her visit, nor did she remember any of the conversations we had that day or the prayers we said together with our family in the recovery room.

I posted this update the following Monday:

[January 15, 2018]

Here's an update on Becky's surgery and recovery. Her surgery was early Friday and took almost four hours. The surgeon indicated it went very well. They removed a large tumor. A week prior it was 5"x5"x4", and she indicated it had grown larger in the last week. The best news was that it hadn't attached to any internal organ, except for the ovary, so there were no complications that could have caused additional issues. Recovery has been good but slow, as might be expected following major surgery. We've been giving Becky an A+

for her recovery efforts each day. We're still not sure when she'll be released. It may take another day or two. I'll let Becky fill in more details when she gets back home. We're thankful for the great care she's had and for the many well wishes and prayers you have sent on our behalf.

After a couple more days of recuperation and observation, the doctors let her go home.

[January 18, 2018]

Dear Friends,

I heartily concur with Dorothy from The Wizard of Oz when she says, "There's no place like home!" It's wonderful to be back in familiar and comfortable surroundings again!

My surgery outcome was, as my doctor termed, a best-case-scenario. She and her team were able to remove all visible signs of cancer. In two weeks I will begin a targeted drug therapy called Rubraca. This is a relatively new FDA-approved treatment for ovarian cancer patients with the BRCA gene mutation who have already gone through two or more rounds of chemotherapy. I guess that's me!

My hospital stay was my first in-patient experience since Ryan was born 28 years ago. I cannot say enough wonderful things about my nursing care! Throughout my five-night stay, nurses and CNAs anticipated my needs and made my stay as comfortable as possible. I had no idea how hard nurses work! One of the coolest things was being cared for by two of my former students! I was so proud of how professional and compassionate this young man and woman have become. So, thank you to my many friends who are nurses, and to all the hospital nursing staffs everywhere for serving as unsung heroes in this profession!

Each round of cancer brings with it a reality check. I blindly jumped into chemotherapy after the first diagnosis and barely had time to digest what was happening before I was in a two-year remission. While in remission, I became hopeful that I was cured. Round two of cancer dashed those hopes. It was also the beginning of me questioning whether chemotherapy was my best long-term treatment option. Midway through round two of chemo, I adopted a holistic approach to living with cancer. Once again, I was hopeful that clean living would cure the cancer. My nine-month remission was wonderful, but it also came to an end! As I face ovarian cancer for the third time, I'm struggling to be hopeful.

Chemo didn't cure my cancer, nor did dietary changes. It's likely that targeted drug therapy will buy me some time, but at what expense? The potential side-effects could lead to a diminished quality of life, and I really don't like pain and discomfort! My mind is spinning with anxiety about my future. I don't like living in this funk! Forgive me, Lord, for this incessant worry!

The WELS online devotion from January 17 reminded me that God, through His Word, doesn't tell me specifically how to make decisions relating to my cancer. The Bible does say whatever we do, we are to do for the glory of God. God doesn't say that I will avoid pain and suffering. He does promise to work everything out for the eternal good of those who love Him. He doesn't tell me why I am suffering. He does invite me to find comfort in Him. He doesn't tell me how or when I will die. He does tell me that whoever believes in Jesus will have eternal life. In effect, God continually says to me, "What are you worried about? I've got this!"

Okay, I feel better now! Writing is cathartic. Putting my thoughts on paper helps me process my healthy emotions and eliminate the ones that bring me down! God has richly blessed my earthly life. From day one, I've tried to include cancer on that list of blessings. As I heal from surgery and move forward with the next round of treatment, I am so looking forward to quality time with family and friends! I can't wait to get back into my weekly teaching rotation with my grandchildren. It won't be long until I can cradle two new grandbabies in my arms. All of this by the side of my wonderful husband who completes me as we travel this journey together.

I am indeed blessed! My hope is built on nothing less than Jesus' blood and righteousness.

Becky was discharged from the hospital on Wednesday morning, January 17, 2018. She was still very weak from her surgery, but she was determined to get out walking again. That afternoon, we went out into our hilly neighborhood and walked down the hill half a block before we went back home. The following day, we went up and down an entire block, and did that twice the next day. After ten days at home, Becky started walking two miles every day and was feeling much better. She was healing physically from her surgery and healing emotionally as well.

During the following month, Becky didn't post any updates on Facebook. She was working through some decisions and wasn't ready to make them public. However, she was researching and consulting with family regarding her next steps in this long cancer journey.

The following are excerpts from a letter Becky sent to her children and their families on January 27, 2018:

Hi Family,

I'm now two weeks out from surgery. It's pretty amazing how our bodies heal! I don't have any pain related to the incision. I have good muscle control in my abs. I sleep well and all my systems are up and running. Dad and I have been walking outside. We started with short walks up and down the hills in our neighborhood until yesterday when we did our normal two-mile walk. Today I walked two miles on my own. The pace is a little slower, but it still feels great!

We had a good visit with Dr. W about Rubraca, the oral drug therapy she is recommending. Dad and I had read up on it before the appointment so we had some prior knowledge and were prepared to ask questions. Dr. W said that within two or three months it's apparent whether or not the drug is going to shrink the tumors. If the tumors are shrinking, you stay on it; if the tumors aren't shrinking, the drug isn't going to work and you try something else. If my cancer is Rubraca-sensitive, the drug will hold the cancer at bay. For how long is anyone's guess, but nine months and beyond is a reasonable expectation. If my cancer doesn't respond to the Rubraca, the cancer will most likely return in three to six months, approximately the same amount of time if we didn't do anything.

Dr. W said she has never had a patient stop taking Rubraca because the body couldn't handle it. Targeted-drug therapy is not hard on the liver and kidneys like systemic chemotherapy. The most common side effects are mild nausea and/or fatigue. We won't know how I will respond until I try it. I experienced comparatively mild side effects from chemo, so maybe I will be fortunate the same way with Rubraca. Bottom line, I feel comfortable moving forward with this treatment.

But you know me, I don't want to make this too simple! So, before making a final decision, I have an appointment for a second opinion with Dr. K (DO) in Mankato. I want to find out what his natural approach to treating my cancer would be. Dr. W. was supportive of getting a second opinion. In fact, she said, "There are many unknowns with cancer treatment Why not come at it from multiple angles?

So, there you have it! I am thankful that my recovery is going well and that I am operating at a normal energy levels. My prayer is that God will guide me in making decisions for treatment and then bless those decisions according to His will for my life. I am in good spirits and thankful for each day of grace given me!

Love, Mom

Her plans to move forward took solid shape shortly thereafter. She visited Dr. K and sent a long note to our extended family, including parents and siblings, on February 2, 2019:

Dear Family,

It's a crisp, sunny morning here in La Crescent. The temps fell below zero overnight, but our thermometer now registers a balmy seven degrees! Glenn and I have been getting outside on a regular basis for a two-mile walk through the hilly neighborhoods of our picturesque town. It feels especially good to have the sun shine down on our pale winter faces!

My recovery from surgery continues on course. It's hard to believe it's only been three weeks. The only residual issues from surgery seem to be a lack of appetite and a foggy memory once in a while. My doctor said it's not uncommon to experience these symptoms after surgery. To me, both the low-grade nausea and foggy head remind me of chemo side effects.

I am ready to start an oral chemo drug called Rubraca. In the meantime, I had an appointment in Mankato, MN, with Dr. K to get a second opinion regarding treatment. I had met him last April but, at that time, had decided to focus on introducing my other lifestyle changes.

This was my first exposure to a Doctor of Osteopathic Medicine (DO). Both a DO and an MD are graduates of medical school. As I understand the difference between the two, an MD is trained to treat the symptoms of an illness, while a DO will seek answers as to why the body's immune system has failed and allowed the cancer to thrive. The DO's treatment plan goes beyond fighting the tumors to repairing the immune system so that the cancer cannot survive and grow. Much of what DO's do is preventative medicine.

I arrived early for my appointment and was reading a magazine in the reception area as I waited. Suddenly I heard a voice say, "Señora!" I looked up and was surprised to see one of my former students from Luther. "Cameron, what are you doing here?" I asked. He replied, "I work here" and, with a little more explanation, "I'm dating the boss's daughter!" Turns out Cameron attended a film camp at Bethany College the summer before his senior year of high school. He met Dr. K's daughter at this film camp and they have been dating ever since! He now works as a medical assistant in the office. I ended up being cared for by two former students while in the hospital and I paid my bill to another former student at Dr. K's office. What a small world!

After some initial tests, Dr. K said I am a very healthy person – with the exception of cancer. My cell health is unusually strong for someone with cancer who has undergone chemotherapy (twice) and had recent major surgery. My diet and regular exercise contribute to cell health. So I asked him, "If I am so healthy, why did I get cancer?" Dr. K said:

1. It's possible environmental factors cause the cancer to turn on in a person with a gene mutation.
2. Nagalase, an enzyme that is created by cancer cells, cloaks the cells and prevents their detection by the immune system. This is the reason that someone like me can have a strong functioning immune system and still be growing a tumor. I had a blood test to identify my current Nagalase level. I'll get the results soon.
3. I should proceed with Rubraca. Reducing the Nagalase level while taking Rubraca will make the Rubraca more effective.

I'm glad I got a second opinion. I am relieved that neither Dr. W nor Dr. K made my treatment decision an either/or proposition, but rather a collaborative one. I have been praying that God would make things clear to me regarding treatment options and He has answered that prayer by giving me some reasonable options. I am at peace moving forward with Rubraca as well as considering the treatment options that Dr. K proposes. In all honesty, I am weary of thinking about, worrying about and talking about cancer. I'm ready to move forward with the next phase of this journey and watch it play out according to God's plan for my life!

Well, there you have it! Glenn continues to take good care of me and we thank God for each and every day!

Love, Mom, daughter, sister

Becky had done a lot of work crafting a plan for what she wanted to do. She knew chemo wasn't going to cure her; she knew her diet wasn't going to cure her. She was okay with the fact that her cancer would almost assuredly return, possibly soon. But there were still options and there was still hope. Because of the research she had done, she wanted to try some new and different things. Rubraca was a newer, daily oral chemo pill which had shown promise for women in her situation who had already gone through platinum-based chemo treatments. She wondered if the treatments to deal with the Nagalase might also be effective.

I remember those days as being unsettling. We went back and forth between being comfortable with God's plan for our lives and then hoping for a lengthy remission if the new treatments worked. It's similar to how the Apostle Paul struggled with living and dying. As he succinctly said, **to me, to live is Christ but to die is gain (Phil 1:21).** The will to keep living is strong, even though we know we have something far better waiting for us in heaven.

It wasn't always easy accepting God's plan for us while hoping for a change in Becky's outlook. Emotionally and spiritually, it seemed the two hopes were incompatible. For my own sanity, accepting God's plan was the only way I could look at our situation. I knew there was a worst-case and a best-case scenario for our lives. Merely hoping and praying for a best-case scenario would only make it harder for me. In the end, I was grateful I could leave all my cares regarding Becky's health in God's hands and allow that His will would be done. That was good enough for me.

A few weeks later, Becky updated her Facebook family regarding her treatment status.

[February 20, 2018]

Dear Friends,

I have found that one of the most difficult aspects of living with cancer is making decisions about treatment. Following the initial diagnosis in 2014, my oncologist summarized my condition with these words: "Your cancer is inoperable, incurable, but treatable. Glenn and I responded, "Okay, tell us what to do next." This is a very common response to an initial cancer diagnosis because the news usually comes out of nowhere and the recipients of the news often have no previous cancer knowledge to fall back on. In your shocked and scared state, you do what the doctor recommends.

Our cancer journey began with the standard of care for ovarian cancer – six rounds of chemotherapy, once every three weeks. Along the way, family members and friends gave me books to read, shared cancer documentaries, and recommended alternative cancer treatment protocols to which I politely said, "Thank you, but I'm comfortable with my current treatment plan." And I was comfortable, until the cancer recurred two years later. When the cancer returned, I began to have second thoughts about the long-term effectiveness of chemotherapy.

The standard of care for the first recurrence of ovarian cancer is six more rounds of chemotherapy. I swallowed hard and began to visit the infusion chair once again every three weeks. The treatment side effects were more noticeable this time. Coupled with the knowledge that chemo wasn't going to cure my cancer, I began to investigate alternative cancer treatments. I was fascinated by what I learned about the connection between diet and cancer. I was also interested in learning about the immune system and the ability of the body to heal itself. I made the decision to suspend the chemo treatments with three of the recommended six infusions remaining. I adopted an anti-cancer diet and wholeheartedly embraced this new way of life.

Nine months later the cancer returned. Round three! Here I am, once again, faced with treatment decisions. For the first time in this journey the tumors were operable so I opted to have surgery. Thankfully, all visible signs of tumors were removed. I am almost six weeks out from surgery and have resumed normal activities. It amazes me how our bodies heal from the invasiveness of major surgery! We are indeed fearfully and wonderfully made.

Ten days ago I began an oral chemo protocol called Rubraca. I am struggling with this, emotionally more than physically. The main side effects are a queasy stomach and a diminished appetite, both manageable from a quality-of-life standpoint. However, I am finding that the constant queasiness messes with my emotions. It's a daily reminder that I have cancer, and I don't want to think about cancer all the time! I also struggle with the fact that this oral drug therapy is designed to continue until it is no longer effective, meaning the cancer has come back.

The median time frame for the effectiveness of this drug is a little over nine months. I ask myself, "What am I doing? Do I really want to feel queasy for the next nine months just to have the cancer come back?" This is hard! While I question many things about chemotherapy, after weighing the pros and cons, I feel that for me right now, this is a reasonable option.

Three weeks ago, I got a second opinion from a doctor of osteopathy (DO). The DO will seek answers as to why the body's immune system has failed and allowed the cancer to thrive. The treatment plan goes beyond removing the tumors to repairing the immune system so that the cancer cannot continue to grow as easily.

In conjunction with Rubraca, I have decided to follow a three-month protocol recommended by my DO that will uncloak the cancer so that both the immune system and the chemo will recognize it and therefore be more effective in attacking it. This Orasal protocol, which I began yesterday, is one that can coincide with chemotherapy. It is also a protocol that should be followed in conjunction with an alkaline diet. This works out perfectly for me because I already follow an alkaline diet!

I guess you could say that I've decided to follow a hybrid treatment plan – the chemo piece from conventional medicine and the Orasal protocol and alkaline diet from the alternative side of things. Both doctors are supportive of melding the two treatments. My oncologist said, "We don't have all the answers so why not come at the cancer from as many different angles as possible!"

It's really easy to be consumed by this cancer journey, to let worries and anxieties about treatment decisions preoccupy my thoughts. I pray every day that God will forgive my lack of trust and replace it with contentment and thanksgiving for all the blessings He daily showers on me, cancer included! I am relieved that my hybrid treatment plan has been implemented and I look forward to getting back into a routine. I call it the new normal. I ask for your prayers that God will bless the treatment plan according to His will for my life. Most importantly, as God's redeemed child, I find my peace in knowing that while I have struggles here on this earth due to a flawed physical body, Jesus has provided complete healing for my soul and has prepared a home for me in heaven!

We have all things, Christ possessing:
Life eternal, second birth,
Present pardon, peace and blessing
While we tarry here on earth;

And by faith's anticipation,
Foretaste of the joy above
Freely giv'n us with salvation
By the Father in His love. **(ELH 484:2)**

Becky continued to teach her grandchildren throughout her oral chemo and alternative protocols. The time spent with her children and grandchildren was precious!

[March 10, 2018]

It was a good day, a little crazy at times, but good!

Becky and I were approached by our pastor early in 2018. He asked if we'd be interested in talking at our church about our cancer journey. We agreed to do that and put together a talk entitled: *Not My Plan - Purposeful Living in the Face of a Terminal Cancer Diagnosis.* In March, 2018, we had the opportunity to share that story with many people. We talked about Becky's cancer journey and how, even though it wasn't exactly what we had planned for our lives, this was God's plan for us. We talked about how God's Word made a huge difference in our ability to deal with the situation. We talked about how God had used this challenge as a blessing in our lives. Finally, we talked about the promises God has made to each of us, how He has known from the beginning the number of days in our lives and how He has prepared a home for us in heaven.

One of the topics I talked about was how the cancer journey affected our family as a whole. I noted the cares and concerns I had as Becky's primary caregiver, and the selfish thoughts of what would happen in my life when Becky dies.

After the presentation, a lady from the congregation, who had lost her husband around 10 years prior, came up to me and said, "It's okay to be selfish. We need to look out for ourselves as well and take care of our own needs, too!" I had never thought about that. I had always been comforted knowing that God's perfect will was sufficient (Psalm 18:30), that He has stated we are His no matter what (Isaiah 43:1), that He has known the days of our lives before we were born (Psalm 139:16), that He wants us to trust Him as our God (Psalm 46:10). But her comment helped me understand that beyond the needs of our loved one who is dealing with the illness, we still need to deal with our lives as well. It was good to be reminded that it was okay to take time to make sure my own needs were also being addressed. After that, even though I still focused a great deal on Becky's needs, I didn't feel guilty when I was focused more inward than not. And that was nice to know!

Finally, the day came when the first part of Becky's 2018 wish list arrived!

[April 1, 2018]

We are so happy to announce the birth of our eighth grandchild, Paul Gerhardt Faugstad, born March 31, 2018. Rejoicing with parents, Peter and Kristin for this new gift of life.

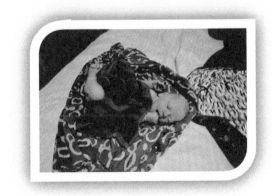

Not long after, part two of Becky's 2018 wish list arrived!

[April 18, 2018]

Elsiana Rebecca Lukasek, born April 17, at 2:12 a.m., 7 lbs. 7 oz, 20.5 inches long. Elsie Madson was her great-great-grandmother. Ana is a variation of her Grandma Lukasek's middle name (Ann), and Rebecca is her Grandma Lussky's name. We are so thankful for this sweet, healthy gift from the Lord!

A short time later, we were able to celebrate another birthday for Becky!

[April 28, 2018]

Dear Friends,

Thank you for the wonderful birthday greetings! I am in awe that I have just celebrated another birthday. A year ago at this time I made the decision to

suspend my last three chemo infusions in favor of an anti-cancer diet and life-style. Best decision ever! Okay, the cancer did recur this past January so these lifestyle changes didn't bring about a complete cure, but I love my quality of life. I sleep well at night and have a lot of energy during the day.

It was also a year ago at the end of May that I closed the door on my teaching career. It was bittersweet to say goodbye to my life at Luther, but oh, the doors God has opened for me with my grandchildren to fill that void! I have healed completely from the tumor-debulking surgery in January. Dosage reductions in the oral chemo drug I am taking have minimized the side effects to the point that I really don't have any!

When I was a young mom, Glenn and I lived far away from family support. How I longed to have my mom close by to give me a break, to have grandparents close by to dote on their grandchildren. How thankful I am that I now have the opportunity as mom to help our daughters and as grandma to be a regular part of our grandchildren's lives. Blessings abound!

I will have three-month check-ups with both my doctors at the end of May. In the meantime, I have no symptoms that indicate the cancer is active.

Living in the shadow of cancer gives me reason to pause and reflect each and every day on the immeasurable temporal and spiritual blessings showered upon me by my gracious God. **Lamentations 3:22-23: The steadfast love of the Lord never ceases; his mercies never come to an end; they are new every morning; great is your faithfulness.**

Country singer and songwriter Keith Urban recorded a song entitled *Making Memories of Us*. Ever since I first heard that song, I've been struck by the importance of making memories with the special people in my life. Even though I never went through married life with Becky consciously thinking about it, we had been making memories since our very first date. Over the years, I've come to learn that shared memories and experiences often form the core of close relationships, whether they be with a spouse or with friends.

Because of that song, I've become more aware of the need to make memories through shared experiences with my wife, family and friends. That's what Becky loved to do.

I think that's one of the reasons Becky loved hosting her students in our home for special events while she was a teacher at Luther High School. For many years, we hosted the drama cast party. Every year, we hosted at least one of her classes for a Spanish-themed dinner. Occasionally, there were other groups that came by as well. Most of the time, these events involved feeding the students as well. I'm quite sure the students also enjoyed that part of those get-togethers!

In May, we were honored to have the Luther High School select choir, Sound Foundation, come over for a night of dinner and music. Everyone had so much fun, but especially Becky. As much as she enjoyed interacting with and having fun with her students in the classroom, she loved how these special events created stronger bonds of friendship that would stand the test of time and distance. On this night, Becky was in her element, feeding her students, listening to their music, making memories, and connecting with each of them!

[May 13, 2018]

> I want to thank the mothers of Luther Sound Foundation students for sharing their sons and daughters with me this Mother's Day evening. I was treated to a private three-hour concert in our living room. The kids literally had to sing for their supper! I provided tacos and sundaes, they provided the beautiful music. Unbelievable talent! I love these kids and their leader, Mr. Adickes.

One of the parents responded to Becky: "Thank you, Mrs. Lussky, for opening your home to them. You have been an incredible influence on them in so many ways."

By late June and early July, we were pretty sure Becky's oral chemo wasn't working. Once again, she was feeling extra bloating in her abdomen, a sign the cancer was back. We knew we were running out of options for treatment, especially if she was unwilling to try the intravenous chemo again. As a result, we both felt a renewed sense of urgency regarding the time we had left to spend together. We wanted every moment to be wonderful. We wanted all of our time together to be special.

In an effort to accommodate Becky's wishes, the entire family went up to the lake for a long weekend together. And Becky, the 58-year-old grandmother of nine and four-time cancer survivor with an active tumor, wanted to get up on one ski one more time and slalom around the lake! And so she did. She never learned to get up on two skis, so she had to get up on one. It took her a few tries, but she finally made it up and slalomed around the lake!

After everyone had left, Becky and I had a few days to ourselves at the lake. We wanted a special picture of the two of us. I propped the tripod in the boat, set the timer on the camera, pressed the shutter, and hopped out onto the dock. This became one of our favorite final lake pictures.

[July 16, 2018]

Dear Friends,

One of the books I read to our grandchildren is called *Jonathan James and the Whatif Monster*. The sneaky Whatif Monster whispers into Jonathan James' ear and fills his head with worries and doubts. I can relate!

Jonathan James isn't the only one that has to deal with the Whatif Monster. This sneaky little guy likes to mess with me as well. Following a blood test several weeks ago my doctor told me that my CA125 level was on the rise, an indication that my cancer was waking up. The very first thought that popped into my head was, "What if we had gotten a complete water filtration system in our house?" It was such a bizarre thought that came out of nowhere! The "what ifs" continued to bombard me. What if I had not requested a dosage reduction in the oral chemo drug I was taking? Would I still be in remission? What if I had done vitamin C infusions? What if I had stopped using hairspray? What if? The list is endless when it comes to the recommendations for curing cancer. Bottom line for me is that the cancer is back, regardless of what I have or have not done to keep it away. It's not my plan, but my friend reminded me that God, in his almighty wisdom, knows exactly what's best for me!

A CT scan last week confirmed a five-inch tumor in my pelvis, enlarged lymph nodes around my heart, stomach and pancreas, and tumor nodules on my colon. I'm not going to lie, it's hard to get this news. I cry. I visualize my funeral. I feel guilty for wanting to live. Shouldn't I desire heaven? Ironically, it's because of cancer that I have this strong desire to live. An early retirement has allowed me to enjoy treasured time with my family. Honestly, it's been the best year of my life! I pray that God will grant me more time to be a wife, mother and grandmother.

And then there are decisions to make about treatment. I said I would never do chemo again. Note to self: never say never. Rubraca, the parp inhibitor, didn't prevent the cancer from recurring. My doctor believes that because my cancer is platinum sensitive, IV chemotherapy can once again be effective in shrinking the tumors. I've decided to go that route, thankful that I still have treatment options. I pray that God will grant healing according to His will for my life.

And so, my cancer journey continues. Obviously, it's a physical journey. But it's also a spiritual journey. I find so much comfort in St. Paul's words when he poses this what if: **1 Corinthians 15:17; 20-22: And if Christ has not been raised, your faith is futile and you are still in your sins. But in fact Christ has been raised from the dead, the first fruits of those who have fallen asleep. For as in Adam all die, so also in Christ shall all be made alive.** My body will die one day, but because Christ rose from the dead, I, too, will rise again. No what ifs there! **1 Corinthians 15:57: Thanks be to God! He gives us the victory through our Lord, Jesus Christ!**

Thank you for your continued prayers. My family and I appreciate your spiritual encouragement as you share Bible passages, hymn verses, devotions, etc. We have God's promises that the Holy Spirit will work through the Word to strengthen us in our faith.

This news from our doctor wasn't totally unexpected, but Becky's cancer was more advanced than we thought it would be. Despite using the oral chemo drug, Becky's cancer had reorganized and redeveloped, evidenced by another five-inch tumor in her lower abdomen. The doctor encouraged us to consider IV chemo treatments again, since it had been effective in the past. Since early 2017, Becky had always said she would never try IV chemo again. I was surprised when she quickly responded to the doctor that she'd be willing to do the chemo once again. I was thankful as well. I think we both knew this was the best chance Becky would have to get some extra time with her loved ones. Becky knew there would be side effects, but she also felt that if it worked, it would be worth it. Becky was thankful for all her earthly blessings, and it was difficult for her to let them go.

[July 17, 2018]

LIFE ISNT ABOUT WAITING FOR THE STORM TO PASS; IT'S ABOUT LEARNING TO DANCE IN THE RAIN. These words are stenciled on the wall of one of the infusion rooms at Gundersen Clinic where I spent the morning today. The quote brought back memories of a rainy day in Florida that perfectly illustrates the point of the quote.

Two years ago, during Spring Break 2016, we visited my brother and sister-in-law at their beach-front condo in Destin, FL. My swimsuit was packed and I couldn't wait to relax on the beach and soak up the warm rays of the sun. It was raining the day we arrived. The next day the rain and wind were even worse! My meteorologist husband said the band of precipitation was stalled over us for the long haul.

I wasn't going to let a little tropical storm deter me from dipping my toes in the warm Gulf waters for the first time in my life, so I sweet-talked my dubious husband into donning his suit and we headed for the beach in the middle of a rainstorm with Lisa, our trusty photographer, in tow. We were determined to document the event! I doubt there are too many meteorologists who have been photographed wading in the ocean during a lightning strike! But since we were leaving the following day, we didn't have time to wait for the storm to pass. We decided to dance in the rain!

I have made it a point to dance in the rain while living with cancer, especially since it's uncertain if the storm will pass. My philosophy from the beginning has been to approach each day with the following attitude: since I'm alive today, I will live life to the fullest. I will pour my heart into teaching before retirement. I will make treasured memories with my family and friends. When my health makes it difficult to dance in the rain according to Plan A, I will move to Plan B and modify my dance.

This morning during my chemo infusion, I read a devotion that discussed finding a balance between loving life and longing for heaven. Peter, my son-in-law, gave me a devotional book entitled *Manual of Comfort* written in Latin in 1611 by John Gerhard and more recently translated into English. The devotions were written following the death of Gerhard's infant son and wife. He gets death and dying! The first devotion immediately spoke to me. In summary, the devotion is a beautiful reminder that God the Father created me, Christ the Son redeemed me from sin, and God the Holy Spirit brought me to faith, not to live forever in this imperfect world, not to be happy for a little while here on earth, but for the blessed and eternal life waiting for me in heaven! Dancing in the rain during my cancer journey can't begin to compare with the glories of being with Jesus forever in heaven.

Jesus died for my transgressions,
All my sins on Him were laid.
He has won for me salvation,
On the cross my debt was paid.
From the grave I shall arise
And shall meet Him in the skies.
Death itself is transitory,
I shall lift my head in glory. **(ELH 354:5)**

Becky's brother and wife, Dan and Lisa, were there when Becky and I first started dating. We spent time in their apartment after our first date. Through the years, Dan and Lisa were blessed in their lives through Lisa's success in Mary Kay. Knowing that Becky had always wanted to attend the annual Mary Kay Seminar in Dallas, TX, Lisa and Dan invited us to join them in early August, 2018.

During Becky's ovarian cancer journey, Lisa had consistently shared Becky's story with her large Mary Kay family. As a result, Becky had been showered with encouragement and prayers from that group of ladies. Many of Lisa's people got to know Becky and see her faith in action. Ultimately, many of them became a part of our Facebook family as well. We were thankful to Lisa and her Unit for their prayers and support.

Before we went to Seminar, Lisa had asked Becky if she'd be willing to speak to her people at their annual awards dinner in Dallas. It was unusual to have somebody who wasn't actually part of Mary Kay speak at an event like this. However, Lisa and Becky knew that what she had to share was important, and Becky relished the chance to say thank you for all the support they had given her.

Following are excerpts from Becky's speech at the Madson Area Event in Dallas:

Hello! It's so great to be here with all you beautiful women. I'm feeling kind of pretty myself tonight. I've always wanted an excuse to wear a glitzy dress like this one.

When Lisa confirmed that we were invited to join them at Seminar, I was *so* excited! Aside from the thrill of celebrating you all in the Madson Unit, I was also pretty pumped that I would get the chance to be glamorous for a couple of days. So here I am, decked out in sequins and lace. I'm terribly honored to be here tonight as the guest of my dear sister and friend!

For the past 32 years, I have watched with awe as Lisa has consistently set goals and then met and exceeded them. God has perfectly equipped Lisa for her Mary Kay career. I know her greatest joy is motivating each of you to achieve your goals and realize your dreams.

Achieving goals to realize our dreams takes planning. I like to plan because I like to be in control. Four years ago, my husband and I started making plans when we determined we had six more years until retirement. Our plans were not God's plans, however. In August, 2014, I was diagnosed with stage 4 ovarian cancer. A few days after my diagnosis, Glenn and I were sitting around the kitchen table. I asked him how he was doing. He replied with a wry smile, "I think I liked our plan better." Whether it's cancer or other challenges in life, what a blessing to know we can make our plans, but the Lord determines our steps.

Living with cancer has made me very mindful of the blessings of life and how important each and every day is. I call it purposeful living. As Mary Kay beauty consultants and Sales Directors, I encourage you to also embrace purposeful living. As someone living with cancer, I can tell you first hand that feeling pretty goes a long way to helping me cope with the physical discomforts that come during treatment and the emotional ups and downs that are a part of living with a terminal illness. My Mary Kay products make me feel pretty every single day!

Lisa has shared my cancer journey with you all, and many of you have reached out to me through Facebook. You've sent cards, gifts, and most importantly, you've prayed for me. I am humbled by this outpouring of love, and tonight I want to say thank you. Thank you for taking the time to encourage me during this challenging time of my life. On more than one occasion, I have texted Lisa, "I just received a card/gift/message from so-and-so. Is she one of yours? Tell me about her."

At the same time, cancer has given me the opportunity to encourage one of your own. When Jessica was diagnosed with colon cancer this past September, Lisa asked me to connect with her. Since that time, Jess and I have had the opportunity to encourage each other and pray for each other while dealing with our respective cancers. It was the coolest thing to meet Jess for the first time at the luncheon in Lisa's suite on Wednesday.

I hope and pray that Seminar 2018 motivates and encourages you, both professionally and personally as you grow your Mary Kay businesses and make a difference in the lives of people around you. You have made a difference in my life! Thank you from the bottom of my heart! May God richly bless each of you!

I didn't know what she was going to say that evening. She worked on her speech without any input from me. I was incredibly proud of her that evening for the impact I knew she had had on many of these women's lives, both professionally and spiritually. It was a wonderful and emotional time for both of us, especially when the large group stood to applaud after she finished! She received a pretty big hug from her husband when she stepped down from the stage that evening.

When we returned home from Dallas, it was back to real life. After a few days in Dallas at a Mary Kay seminar, with many pretty women dressed up in beautiful clothes, Becky seemed more focused on beauty and how she looked and what that all meant in the eternal scheme of things. You'll see how that played out in her mind in her post the day after we got home.

[August 8, 2018]

Dear Friends,

I have a confession to make: I have always been conscious of my looks in an insecure way. When we were first married, I vividly recall the time standing at the bathroom mirror with Glenn by my side and saying, "I'm so ugly." I will never forget what Glenn said to me, "You are insulting my taste. I think you look beautiful!" You can be sure I never again verbalized those negative thoughts around Glenn, but unfortunately, I still internalized them. I was constantly dieting. I hated my hair. I felt frumpy in my choice of clothes. What a waste of mental energy!

Fast forward to my cancer diagnosis four years ago. I vowed to myself that I was going to be a pretty cancer patient. I embraced my initial hair loss because I had never liked my hair! I loved my wig. For the first time in my life I felt that my hair was pretty! When my hair grew back, I fell in love with the pixie cut and I still love my hair. A year ago, I adopted an anti-cancer diet. Not only did I lose 20 pounds, but the best part is that I have been freed from food cravings. I no longer binge on 1 lb. bags of M&M's and Skittles. In fact, it's impossible to binge eat because everything I eat is good for me. I feel *so* good physically and emotionally.

While living with cancer, it has been important for me to feel pretty. I wear make-up every day. Though I'm no longer teaching, I make it a point to dress in cute clothes even if I'm just hanging around the house. These personal grooming touches really help me stay positive. I suppose this could be chalked up to vanity, but I'm okay with that. It's a positive coping mechanism for me in the ugly world of cancer.

Glenn and I recently attended the Mary Kay Seminar in Dallas with my brother Dan and his wife Lisa, who is a National Sales Director. I had so much fun wearing glitzy dresses and feeling glamorous. In my speech to Lisa's Sales Directors and beauty consultants, I told them how much fun it was to have an excuse to wear a lacy sequined dress. It made me feel pretty.

Following my speech, Lisa recognized the members of the Madson Area for their accomplishments throughout the Seminar year. Jackie, one of Lisa's Sales Directors, accepted her award and then looked right at me and said, "Becky, I give you permission to wear your beautiful lacy sequined dress to your next chemo infusion on Tuesday!" So, guess what? I did just that! And I felt pretty. Thank you, Jackie, for encouraging me with your unexpected suggestion.

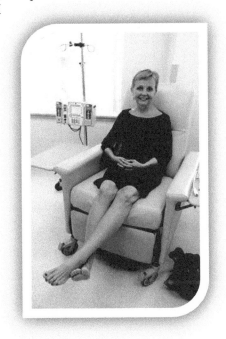

Feeling pretty goes only skin deep, however. I know that my spiritual nature is ugly with sin and there is nothing I can do to make it pretty. The Bible says in **Psalm 51:5: Surely I was sinful at birth, sinful from the time my mother conceived me.** Those are some harsh words about my natural state. St. Paul reminds me in **Ephesians 2:1: You were dead in your trespasses and sins.** Nothing pretty there, either!

Such words could lead me to despair, but our gracious God doesn't want me or you to despair. He uses this clothing analogy to describe who we are in Christ: **Isaiah 61:10: I delight greatly in the LORD; my soul rejoices in my God. For he has clothed me with garments of salvation and arrayed me in a robe of his righteousness.** Christ dressed me in His robe of righteousness when I became His child through the washing of baptism. **Galatians 3:27: For all of you who were baptized into Christ have clothed yourself in Christ.** Feeling pretty in my glitzy dress is temporary. I will live forever in heaven because I wear the robe of Christ's righteousness!

My cancer journey continues. On Tuesday, I had my second chemo infusion. Before each infusion, I have a blood test that shows my CA125 level, the marker for ovarian cancer. In the past, my CA125 number has always gone down markedly after the first infusion. This time it was elevated. My doctor had some plausible explanations for why this could have happened and cautioned us not to judge the efficacy of the treatment solely on the CA125 level. She said the greatest measure of whether or not treatment is working is how I feel.

And how do I feel? I feel normal! I experienced three days of mild fatigue following the first infusion, but that has been followed by two weeks of high energy, healthy appetite and restful sleep. Sometimes it's hard to grasp that I'm living with cancer when throughout the course of living with this disease I have been blessed to carry on a normal life. Believe me, I don't take this for granted! Most importantly, I rest securely in the fact that through Christ, I am a forgiven child of God and adorned in His robe of righteousness. To God be the glory!

P.S. I shared with you my insecurities about my looks, not because I am looking for compliments, but because I like to be real and I suspect there are others out there that can relate to my insecurities. Rather than compliments, I desire your prayers and your spiritual encouragement. Most importantly, I pray that the Holy Spirit fills you with the same confidence and hope for heaven that comes through faith in Jesus!

> His robes for mine: O wonderful exchange!
> Clothed in my sin, Christ suffered 'neath God's rage.
> Draped in His righteousness, I'm justified.
> In Christ I live, for in my place He died.
> **(Anderson and Habegger)**

This was a transitional post for Becky. Even though she still felt fairly normal, I think she knew the elevated CA-125 number wasn't a good sign. If the IV chemo wasn't going to work and there were no other treatment options, it was clear to me that Becky was transitioning her thoughts toward her future life in heaven.

I especially like this post because through it, we became familiar with the beautiful song *His Robes for Mine*. We found a number of great versions on YouTube and played them frequently. We found this song to be a beautiful representation of justification, that we are declared righteous before God because of Christ's perfect life and death. Jesus took on our sin and suffered death for us. Knowing and believing that, we are, in turn, clothed in His righteousness and will live eternally in heaven. Becky knew she wanted that song sung at her funeral. That's the message she loved and the message she wanted others to hear.

*C*hapter 12
To Live is Christ, To Die is Gain

[September 2, 2018]

Dear Friends,

While I have been living with cancer these past four years many of you have been praying for me and my family. Thank you! God has faithfully answered our prayers for spiritual strengthening with a resounding *yes*! He has filled me with the peace described by the Apostle Paul in his letter to the Philippians: **Philippians 4:7: And the peace of God, which surpasses all understanding, will guard your hearts and your minds in Christ Jesus.** It's an inexplicable peace.

God has also answered our prayers for physical healing. Early on, I was blessed with a two-year remission. Subsequent recurrences have been halted for a time by medical treatment and lifestyle changes, certainly blessings from God and answers to our prayers. Recently, however, it's become apparent that my cancer has become resistant to medical intervention. Does this mean that God has stopped answering our prayers? Absolutely not! He also answers our prayers with *wait, not now* or *no*. He knows what's best for me!

The disease has progressed in spite of surgery in January, five months on an oral chemo drug and two IV chemo infusions. Last week Glenn and I met with my doctor to discuss further options. Based on that discussion, I have decided to discontinue medical treatment. Surgery is not an option because it's impossible to remove the tumors on my intestine without life-threatening damage to the bowel. Trying new chemo regimens would at best give me several additional months, but with the accompanying side effects. I want to protect my quality of life and that does not include chemo side effects!

The next phase in this journey is palliative care, managing my symptoms and my pain. My doctor has passed me off to the palliative care team at Gundersen. We have our first appointment with them on Wednesday. I will also continue with my anti-cancer lifestyle and implement some new protocols. Since Minnesota is a medical cannabis state, I plan to investigate that option as well.

There is no way of knowing what my life expectancy is at this point and, frankly, it doesn't matter. I plan to continue living one day at a time just as I have throughout this entire cancer journey. Right now, I have discomfort related to the cancer, but it doesn't impede my daily activities. I can feel crummy sitting on the couch or I can push through feeling crummy and attend funerals and weddings, take care of our grandchildren and play host to family and friends. Pretty much a no-brainer in my book!

I cannot say enough about my doctor that has cared for me these past 18 months. She has been compassionate, a good listener and respectful of what I want. At my appointment last week, I thanked her for being so supportive of my wishes. She replied, "You have made a difference in my life by your calm resolve. You changed the way I look at life. I will never forget you!" Wow! I didn't see that coming. This was the opening that I needed to tell her about the hope I have in Jesus. I told her that my calm resolve comes from believing that Jesus is my Savior from sin and knowing that He has prepared a home for me in heaven! All along I have been praying for my doctor.

Now I can be confident that the Holy Spirit has an opening to work in her heart! Such an obvious answer to my prayers!

I am in good spirits and at peace with this decision, but I won't lie, it's hard for me, Glenn and our family as the reality sets in that we are coming down the home stretch. I look forward to heaven but I am anxious about the dying process and how that will play out. I have to trust that God will carry me through just as He has carried me through everything else in my 59 years. Sometimes that's easier said than done. Please continue to pray for me and our family. While we are fully confident that heaven awaits me and all believers, the sadness that accompanies death is also very real. Martha experienced this sadness when her brother Lazarus died. Jesus addressed her sadness when He said to her: **John 11:25-26: I am the resurrection and the life. The one who believes in me will live, even though they die; and whoever lives by believing in me will never die.**

Thanks to Thee, O Christ victorious!
Thanks to Thee, O Lord of Life!
Death hath now no power o'er us,
Thou hast conquered in the strife.
Thanks because Thou didst arise
And hast opened paradise!
None can fully sing the glory
Of the resurrection story.

Thou hast died for my transgression,
All my sins on Thee were laid;
Thou hast won for me salvation,
On the cross my debt was paid.
From the grave I shall arise
And shall meet Thee in the skies.
Death itself is transitory;
I shall lift my head in glory. **(ELH 354:2,5)**

Once again, Becky and I were moved by the love and support of those who left encouraging words.

[September 4, 2018]

Thank you, dear friends, for your encouraging words and continued prayers! God's blessings abound! **Philippians 4:4-7: Rejoice in the Lord always. I will say it again: Rejoice! Let your gentleness be evident to all. The Lord is near. Do not be anxious about**

anything, but in every situation, by prayer and petition, with thanksgiving, present your requests to God. And the peace of God, which transcends all understanding, will guard your hearts and your minds in Christ Jesus.

When we learned from the doctors there was nothing further they could do to combat Becky's cancer, we understood the final phase of our cancer journey had begun. The oral chemo didn't work. The IV chemo didn't work. Becky's cancer was progressing and we knew palliative care was the beginning of the end. We were ready to move into this new phase.

Our daughters, however, were not. Much like their mother, Kristin and Karyn were students of healthy living and healthy lifestyles. They were on the health through nutrition bandwagon long before Becky considered it. They had read numerous articles from many different sources and had their own thoughts regarding things that might still help combat the cancer through natural remedies.

Kristin, in particular, identified a variety of protocols which might help. We agreed to try some of them. Like many other things, including Becky's anti-cancer diet, it's impossible to say how much these protocols helped. But we do know that when she was on them, she felt good. We also know that, in the end, they couldn't stop the cancer from continuing its forward progression. Even so, we were glad we tried them.

Even more, I learned just how much our girls longed for Becky to have more time with them and their children. Becky and I had lived this cancer journey every day for over four years. For the most part, we had come to terms with it and the ultimate conclusion. I think it was harder for our children to accept it. They understood the glories awaiting their mother in heaven, but they didn't have the opportunity to process the daily changes that were occurring like I did. This was a period of transition where we all had to start letting go of the hope that Becky would have more time with us.

In August, Becky and I had been asked to present our *Not My Plan* talk to the Luther High School students and faculty, along with other public guests. We agreed, and on September 11, 2018, we told about our cancer journey and how God gave us strength and contentment on that journey.

From a health perspective, a lot had transpired since we gave the presentation at our church in March. Aside from the updated health status information, our message hadn't changed much.

Acknowledging the challenges associated with terminal cancer, especially as we were heading into its final stages, we were still thankful for the blessings God had showered on us and the promises He had made regarding our future.

Afterward, numerous students, faculty and other friends lined up to give Becky their love and express their support. That was special and meant a lot to her! As one of her former students posted online after the presentation:

"So much respect and love for Señora Lussky! She is such a beautiful soul and an amazing role model for everyone. Te amo mucho."

Around the middle of September, Becky had started feeling the effects of her cancer as it impacted her bowels. The cancer hadn't penetrated the bowels, but there was enough of it in her abdomen to prevent the bowels from being able to work effectively. She had adopted laxative and enema protocols to keep her system moving so it wouldn't get blocked up. She knew that obstructed bowels was one of the main causes of death for ovarian cancer patients.

In normal life, most people don't like to talk about bowel movements and the passing of gas. We take this natural process for granted, until it doesn't work. But let me assure you, when your life depends on the ability to do those things, whenever it happens, there's reason to be thankful! You learn to appreciate those little things.

During this time, we were overwhelmed by incredible kindnesses from many different people. Tom and Robyn, our wonderful friends from Salt Lake City, had thought about coming out to visit. Instead, they sent the money they would have spent on travel to our daughter Karyn, their Goddaughter, so they could use it to make memories with Becky. We took a riverboat cruise with the family and created grandma blankets for each of our grandchildren, adorned with special pictures of them with their grandma.

We also received an incredible photo shoot from one of Becky's former students. Sarah had become one of the premier photographers in our area. She was starting a new non-profit organization which would take remembrance photos for people in our situation. What a wonderful gift!

On September 23, Sarah spent a couple of hours with our entire family, taking beautiful pictures and gifting them to us. Over the last couple of months, when Becky was failing, Sarah also spent time taking other photos and videos and putting together a remembrance video for us. We were incredibly thankful for such a special keepsake gift!

On September 24, 2019, we celebrated our 35th anniversary. Four years prior, I don't think either of us imagined we'd make it to 35 years. God had certainly blessed us! Our children put together a beautiful card commemorating this event and these blessings.

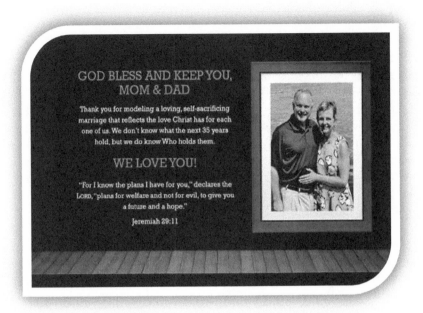

GOD BLESS AND KEEP YOU,
MOM & DAD

Thank you for modeling a loving, self-sacrificing
marriage that reflects the love Christ has for each
one of us. We don't know what the next 35 years
hold, but we do know Who holds them.

WE LOVE YOU!

"For I know the plans I have for you," declares the
LORD, "plans for welfare and not for evil, to give you
a future and a hope."

Jeremiah 29:11

[September 24, 2018]

Happy 35th wedding anniversary to the love of my life! When we pledged to be faithful to each other in sickness and in health, we had no idea that a cancer journey was in our future, but God did. He put the perfect man by my side and equipped him to sustain and support me every step of the way. I am blessed beyond measure. I love you, Glenn!

I feel as though *I* was the one who was blessed. When we talked about it, which we did regularly, we both understood how God had richly blessed us both with one another!

We ate at The Waterfront that evening, one of Becky's favorite local restaurants. While we were there, Becky commented that she wanted to treat all of our adult children to a Waterfront dinner as a special remembrance for all of us.

I remember thinking at the time that if Becky's health kept declining at the same rate as the previous month, she might not be able to eat if we didn't plan the event as soon as possible. I thought back to early August when she was feeling normal. As the month progressed and we left the lake on the 20th, Becky knew she would not return. She could no longer handle the long car ride. By late August, we were working on approvals for her to get medical cannabis for her pain. In early September, we started talking to the funeral home and monument company to start that process. By the middle of September, she was no longer able to go 90 minutes in the car to teach lessons to her grandchildren. Instead, they came to our home.

We coordinated with our children and determined that a November 2 get-together would work for everyone. Extrapolating the changes from the previous five weeks ahead another five weeks, I wondered if she'd be able to handle a dinner out at that time. We planned the evening out in case it would work, but also planned for a nice meal in, just in case it wouldn't work for Becky to go out at that time.

In late September and early October, Becky found it increasingly uncomfortable to sit in a chair. She needed to spend more time lying down. On October 14, after going to Bible Class and church, Becky told me she could no longer spend that much time sitting. She couldn't go to Bible Class anymore. The next week, she said sitting just an hour in church was getting to be too much as well. She attended her last service on October 21, 2018.

In spite of her efforts to keep her bowels moving, she started to have significant problems by the middle of October. Up to that point, her medications had helped with the pain, but she started to get more nauseous during the last half of the month. Anti-nausea medications helped, but it was clear things were going downhill. On October 27, she started having trouble keeping her food and medications down. An inability to eat much or keep her medications down was certainly going to be a problem. Knowing that we would need more help, we officially commenced with Hospice care that day.

[October 27, 2018]

Dear Friends,

I recently realized that something's changed about me. I used to face each day as one who was living. Now I face each day as one who is feeling the physical effects of dying. What happened? Why the change in attitude? Perhaps it's because I *am* dying. The pelvic tumor continues to grow and invade space meant for the intestines which interferes with a number of bodily functions. When people ask how I am doing, I will often respond, "I'm in a slow decline," meaning I still can do most things, but more slowly and requiring much more energy.

Tumors can interfere with bodily functions. They can also cause discomfort and pain. Minnesota is a medical marijuana state. Initially, cannabis was my go-to pain reliever. The cannabis didn't completely knock back the pain, but it took the edge off. That changed last week. Even with the cannabis, the pain was not going away! In consultation with my palliative care nurse, I introduced hydrocodone to my pain management arsenal. I had wanted to avoid opioids for as long as possible because they bring with them their own unique blend of side effects. Thankfully, for a time, I found a balance with cannabis, hydrocodone, Senna and Miralax that kept the pain at bay without constipation. This morning, new side effects surfaced, namely nausea and vomiting. An anti-nausea medication called Zofran stopped the vomiting so that my pain meds could stay in my system. Bottom line, I am in a physical decline and the decline is following the typical stages for ovarian cancer.

That being said, I am in good spirits emotionally. In His Word, God keeps reminding me of His promises for eternal life through faith in Jesus. That excites me! He also promises to be with me as I pass through the valley of the shadow of death. That comforts me! While I'm fearful of the dying process, I'm ready to die. I'm ready to move from this temporary home to my eternal home in heaven. I love this promise of Jesus: **John 14:1-3: Let not your hearts be troubled. Believe in God, believe also in me. In my Father's house are many rooms. If it were not so, would I have told you that I go to prepare a place for you? And if I go and prepare a place for you, I will come again and will take you to myself, that where I am you may be also.** I wonder, "What will my room be like?"

I can't wrap my brain around eternity or perfection. Believing in heaven is the ultimate act of faith. God says it's so; therefore it is! The apostle Paul writes in **2 Corinthians 4:16-18: Therefore we do not lose heart. Though outwardly we are wasting away, yet inwardly we are being renewed day by day. For our light and momentary troubles are achieving for us an eternal glory that far outweighs them all. So we fix our eyes not on what is seen, but on what is unseen, since what is seen is temporary, but what is unseen is eternal**. I am dying. At my death, I will cross over from this temporary life here on earth to my eternal home in heaven. Wow!

Back to the present: I'm not dead yet! It's living while dying that can get tricky. Last week was fairly normal. Glenn and I attended church on Sunday morning. We enjoyed visits from family and friends. Homeschool lessons happened – Lukaseks on Wednesdays and Faugstads on Thursdays. I may sneak in a few more naps during the day, but who's counting?

I have lifted my anti-cancer dietary restrictions. When I do have an appetite, I eat what I crave. I have a few strange cravings: pizza, my mom's lemon angel-food dessert, Ryan's chicken wings and sauces and tortilla chips. What's strange is that I do not crave fruits and vegetables. What's with that after loving my vegetarian diet for so long? Ice Cream isn't on my cravings list either.

No one is giving us any indication of how long I will live. We hear, "Everyone's journey is different." There are times when I scream in my head, "How long is this going to take?" "What is dying going to look like?" I think I want to know. But do I really? There's a reason God doesn't give us all the details about our death and the time leading up to our death. He has a much better plan than I have! I trust that He will get me through this. But in all honesty, when I don't feel well, I'm ready for it to be over. Today is one of those days.

Since suspending treatment at the end of August, Glenn and I have made the most of our time to plan end-of-life issues – funeral, burial, legal documents, insurance. It was fun, in a morbid sort of way, to be able to do this together, in consultation with our friends who work in the funeral industry. What a blessing to make these personal decisions with fellow Christians. We were also blessed to celebrate our 35th wedding anniversary with our immediate family September 22-24. We had no idea as newlyweds how meaningful our vows "in sickness and in health…'til death us do part" would be 35 years later.

God chose the perfect man for me and God is now sustaining him as he puts my needs before his own. You are my rock, Glenn!

Thank you for your continued prayers. People ask what they can specifically pray for. Pray for physical relief from pain, patience to endure the dying process and, most importantly, spiritual strength through God's words of promise. Pray for my family! If you have questions about how I'm doing, feel free to ask! Make me smile with a fun memory you have of us. What I really like is live music so if any of you want to come over and sing or play for me, that would make me smile!

I am coming down the home stretch. The hymn writer says it so well:

> I'm but a stranger here, Heaven is my home;
> Earth is a desert drear; Heaven is my home:
> Danger and sorrow stand, Round me on every hand;
> Heaven is my fatherland, Heaven is my home.
>
> What though the tempest rage, Heaven is my home;
> Short is my pilgrimage, Heaven is my home:
> And time's wild wintry blast, Soon shall be over past;
> I shall reach home at last, Heaven is my home.
>
> There at my Savior's side, Heaven is my home;
> I shall be glorified, Heaven is my home.
> There are the good and blest, Those I love most and best;
> And there I too shall rest, Heaven is my home. **(CW 427:1-3)**

This was to be Becky's last post on Facebook, as she continued to feel worse day by day. She didn't have the energy to sit up, much less put her thoughts down on paper.

Becky noted in this post the visits we had started to receive from family and friends. This had actually started in early September, with special visitors stopping by to spend time with Becky. By the middle of October, as word got out that Becky was declining, more of our friends started scheduling time during the day to visit. Once Becky posted this message, our schedule filled up quickly. Numerous friends offered to come and play music, sing, and even dance for Becky. Once again, we were overwhelmed by the kindnesses and gifts people shared with us.

Becky spent a lot of time lying on the couch, as that was most comfortable for her. Spending time with family was very important, and our children tried to be around as much as they could. October 31st was Becky's last day teaching her grandchildren. After that day, daughter Karyn posted:

[October 31, 2018]

Savoring our time with our wonderful mama and grandma.

I walk with Jesus all the way;
His guidance never fails me;
Within His wounds I find a stay
When Satan's pow'r assails me;
And by His footsteps led,
My path I safely tread.
No evil leads my soul astray;
I walk with Jesus all the way.

My walk is heav'nward all the way;
Await, my soul, the morrow,
When God's good healing shall allay
All suff'ring, sin, and sorrow.
Then, worldly pomp, be gone!
To heav'n I now press on.
For all the world I would not stay;
My walk is heav'nward all the way. **(CW 431:5-6)**

This beautiful hymn reminds us that our earthly walk is beset by problems while our walk with Jesus is toward our home in heaven.

We had many visitors come to our home over the next week. The Luther Sound Foundation made an appearance on November 5. On the evening of November 8, a group of 44 students, former students and parents came by for an event they called *Singing for Señora*. Becky had been struggling considerably on the 7th and 8th, with vomiting becoming a routine part of her day. When the group started arriving outside around 6:45 p.m., Becky was in the middle of one of those episodes. She said, "I don't think they should come in." I asked her if it would be okay if they just came into the adjoining room to sing. She relented.

But once they all came in, Becky perked up like I hadn't seen during the previous few days. This special group of people not only made her day with the music they sang, but they allowed her to have some fun in the process and forget her physical challenges for a while. Afterward, Becky felt well enough to allow almost everyone to stop by her hospice bed and greet her briefly and share a hug. That was a special evening for Becky and, I think, for those who came to sing for her! I noted on Becky's Facebook page:

[November 8, 2018]

> We have been very blessed during the past couple of weeks to have so many wonderful people come and share their time and gifts with Becky! Among them were the Luther High School Sound Foundation and a wonderful group of 44 Luther friends who came by to sing for Becky tonight. I can tell you that everyone who has come has helped lift her spirits with your singing and dancing! Thank you to *everyone* who has shared your gifts with her. The love you have shown her has been a real blessing!

Lisa, who helped organize the singing for Becky, responded, "What a blessing to sing with 44 of the Luther family for Señora Lussky tonight. It's an experience I will never forget! Señora has taught us all about how to live and die with dignity and grace with Christ as the center of it all. Thank you, Glenn, for allowing us into your home and sharing that time with us all."

The following morning, when our Hospice nurse learned the problems had escalated the previous two days, they admitted Becky to the hospital. She hadn't been able to eat much of anything for the prior couple of weeks. We figured the cancer must be obstructing the bowels and that's what the rest of her life would be like.

After they did a scan at the hospital, we were thankful to learn there wasn't an obstruction from cancer. The obstruction was that her system simply was not able to move things through any more and everything was backed up. The doctors hoped they might be able to help, and kept a positive attitude toward her situation.

Those first days were tenuous. Our daughters felt an imminent loss approaching, and started posting on Becky's page:

Kristin: Many of you know that my mom is nearing the end of her earthly life. I've been struggling with grief. Why, God? Why do you allow such suffering? A dear friend shared this quote with me, and it hit home.

"God in His purpose has ordained before the beginning of the world by what crosses and sufferings He would conform every one of His elect to the image of His Son. His cross shall and must work together for good." -Martin Luther

Romans 8:28: And we know that all things work together for good to them that love God, to them who are the called according to his purpose.

> What God ordains is always good:
> This truth remains unshaken.
> Though sorrow, need, or death be mine,
> I shall not be forsaken.
> I fear no harm,
> For with his arm
> He shall embrace and shield me;
> So to my God I yield me. **(CW 429:5)**

Karyn: I've always thought my mom was invincible. I always wanted to be just like her. She is one of the strongest people I know. She is strong in faith, strong in wisdom, strong in constitution and strong in opinions. Perhaps that's why it's so hard to watch you weaken and fade, mom. I'm really going to miss your strength in my life. I'm really going to miss your wisdom and support as I navigate motherhood. I'm really going to miss our conversations about life. I'm even going to miss our conversations about death.

I hate the dying process. I hate seeing you suffer. But I know that something much better awaits you. When God deems the time right, He will take you to the heavenly mansions you have taught me about all these years. By faith alone – not because of anything you've done; by grace alone – not by your own strength, but by God's work through Jesus.

Isaac has been so privileged to have had you as his first piano teacher. Do you know what he has been playing the past few days? This beautiful hymn about heaven:

> Jerusalem the Golden, with milk and honey blessed;
> The sight of it refreshes The weary and oppressed;
> I know not, Oh, I know not, What joys await us there,
> What radiancy of glory, What bliss beyond compare! **(CW 214:1)**

It's such a privilege to have you as my mom, my mentor and my very close friend. I love you!

Two days after her admission to the hospital, I needed to let everyone know what was happening:

[November 11, 2018]

Just to keep you all up to date on how Becky is doing. Some of you may know, but many may not, that Becky was admitted to the hospital Friday morning. During the previous two weeks, she had not been able to eat more than a small bite or two each day due to nausea, and it was increasingly becoming a problem keeping anything down, including her meds and water.

We received good news by late Friday. There was concern her intestines were obstructed by cancer, but that was not the case. However, they were completely blocked up, likely because the cancer was impeding the intestines from moving things through in a normal fashion. Nothing could get through, hence the significant nausea, etc.

The doctors moved all meds to her port and made a little progress trying to clean out her system. All good news. They still want her to be able to take her meds orally and consistently be able to move food through before they release her. We don't know how long that will take, though it will likely be at least a few days, and maybe quite a few more.

She's quite weak after eating so little the past couple of weeks, but is much improved from a couple of days ago. We don't know the timing of God's plans, but we do know the blessings He has in store for her. Thank you for your continued prayers for Becky's comfort, and for our family as well!

While Becky was in the hospital, I slept there almost every night. The hospital pull-out couch wasn't the most comfortable, but it was better being there with Becky than not! I was able to get away for a bit each day to clean up, run errands and take care of things at home.

One of the first days we were there, a devotion we received via email focused on a passage Becky had shared in her last Facebook post: **John 14: 2-3: In my Father's house are many rooms. If it were not so, would I have told you that I go to prepare a place for you? And if I go and prepare a place for you, I will come again and will take you to myself, that where I am you may be also.** Those are profound and meaningful words. They offer incredible assurance from Jesus himself that heaven is real. If it were *not* so, He wouldn't have told us He was going to prepare a place for us! What blessed assurance that is for those who believe in Jesus as their Savior!

My update a number of days later showed there was some improvement, along with some challenges:

[November 16, 2018]

It was an up and down week at the hospital. The doctors and nurses were able to get the bad nausea under control fairly quickly but had a harder time keeping it away. After a number of days with glimmers of hope, the last two days have been more good than bad. Becky has even had an appetite and has eaten real food for a couple of meals.

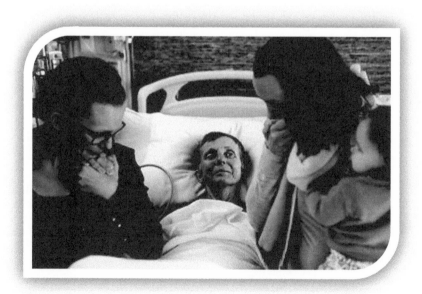

The doctors are now working on a plan which will enable us to keep the current IV meds going at home. We'll test that out over the weekend and, if all goes well, she might be released as early as Monday! She's still very weak, but as long as we can keep her comfortable, I'm sure she'll appreciate the home environment.

While here, we've been showered with well wishes from so many. All your encouragement – the text messages, letters, visits, food, flowers and singing – has meant a lot to Becky. Thank you, everyone, for your kindnesses and prayers.

We were even visited by Brian Davison and Benjamin Lawrenz, members of Koine, in between their appearances at Luther High School. Thank you, Brian and Benjamin, for such a kind gift!

It would be another 10 days before Becky was released from the hospital. In the meantime, there were many tears and goodbyes and opportunities to savor time with family and friends.

Daughter Karyn posted: "I'm thankful for many things and many people, but if I had to choose one thing this year, it would be the bonus time we've had with mom. We didn't know if she would make it to Thanksgiving, but here she is, surprising us every day with little spurts of energy! Amid her weakness and discomfort, she's still making others smile and laugh, and she's always looking for an opportunity to tell just one more person about Jesus."

At this point in Becky's life, that was the most important thing she wanted. Her witness was on her whiteboard in her hospital room. She talked about Jesus and her confidence in heaven with her nurses and doctors and even our family.

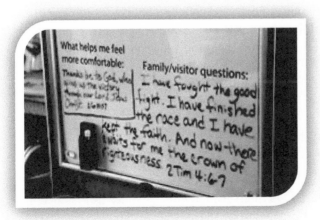

Sister-in-law Lisa put it this way after her visit on the 23rd: "So grateful to be able to visit with my beautiful sister-in-law, Glenn and family members today. She asked me to give her a makeover; it was an honor to do so. When I said goodbye a couple weeks ago, I didn't know that I would get to see her again on this earth. But God's plan was perfect as always. Every time I am in her presence she reminds me of our Savior's love. She said that this phase is very hard, but she talked about Jesus in the Garden of Gethsemane wanting his cup to pass from him and then Pontius Pilate and the scourging, and then the cross for six hours. She says that puts everything into perspective for us as we go through dying and death. Thank you, Becky, for your perspective! I love you!"

Audra, one of Becky's students during her first years of teaching, visited on the 25th. After her visit she posted: "Sometimes there are people in your life that leave more than just memories. They imprint feelings on your heart and soul. This beautiful woman was my Spanish teacher in high school and she was such a person to me. She has been fighting the good fight for years, sharing not just her journey but her love of our Lord all along the way. Tears stream down my face with each post I read. You are so loved and such a faithful servant. 'Oh, the sweet life of a Christian that hath made his peace with God! He is fit for all conditions: for life, for death, for everything'."

Finally, on Tuesday, November 27, we were discharged from the hospital. It was at that time the doctors told me that, when she was admitted, they didn't think she would ever be able to leave the hospital. It was with considerable joy for us and for her doctors when she started to eat real food after 10 days and got a fairly regular appetite back after two weeks. Being discharged 18 days after we arrived was quite an event for us and the nursing staff. They even helped us have a dinner date in her room the evening before, complete with a flower they stole from an arrangement at the nurses' station. We were all happy she could go back home!

Becky had three good days in the week that followed her return home. Even though her system was moving again, the cancer was still progressing. She required increasing amounts of pain and nausea medications to keep her comfortable. By early the following week, she couldn't walk any more, even with a walker. She started to say things that didn't make any sense. Whether it was the cancer or the medications, she couldn't do anything without assistance, and her limited appetite started to wane almost completely.

Our good friend, Kris, is a nurse at Gundersen, where Becky was hospitalized. Kris was such a blessing to us during those last 19 days at home. She organized and coordinated nighttime nursing help from a wonderful group of family and friends who were nurses. That allowed me to take care of things during the day without wearing out. Kris came over every day to help with Becky's care when things got more challenging. As much as I learned in the process of taking care of Becky during those last two months, there were so many areas where I was lost and simply didn't know what to do. The nursing help we received from Kris and others was such an amazing gift and blessing.

It was clear Becky was getting ready to go home to heaven. I went to bed each night not knowing if our nurse helper would wake me during the night to tell me she had died. I had no idea what to expect. I hadn't posted anything for 17 days and, though I knew the days were probably getting short, wanted to provide an update for the many people who followed her on Facebook. I posted on her page:

[December 14, 2018]

> Just a quick update for those wondering. Becky has been back home since November 27. She had a couple of difficult days the first week but we've been able to keep her fairly comfortable most of the time. She continues to fail and is no longer able to get out of bed or even respond most of the time. She is ready to be taken home and is looking forward to it. Thank you all for your continued prayers on our behalf! Glenn

We had planned our family Christmas celebration for December 15. We hoped Becky would be able to interact, but she spent the day sleeping. Still, I think she could hear us and knew I was there when I would hold her hand during the day. She was in the room with us, and I think she knew we were there with her.

Usually, when we moved her around in bed to help her during that last week, it would be very uncomfortable for her. That evening, when we helped her get ready for the overnight, she didn't even respond when we rolled her onto her side. I knew then she was slipping away and was probably not even conscious of anything. In addition, she was no longer able to clear her lungs.

That night was difficult. Even after all we had been through, I still wasn't ready for the emotions that would come with her death. I was up with her all night, holding her hand and making sure her pain medications were maximized so there was no way she would feel any discomfort. We could tell when the end was getting near. Kris had come earlier in the night. Our pastor arrived around 6:25 a.m. When she took her last breaths around 6:45 a.m., it didn't matter how ready I was. It didn't matter that we had been in the grieving process for almost four and a half years, or that we'd had plenty of time to grieve during the last few months, or that we had many moments of closure. That was, to this point, the most difficult moment I've experienced in my life.

Even with all that time to prepare, the reality of a beloved spouse breathing her last breath was overwhelming.

In the weeks leading up to Becky's death, I had been working on her final post. Becky had been a spiritual inspiration to so many during her life, especially during her years with ovarian cancer. I wanted her last post, in post-mortem, to reflect what she would have said, one that would reflect the joy she would be feeling at the time, in heaven with her Savior.

[December 16, 2018]

Hebrews 12:1b-2: Let us run with perseverance the race that is set before us, fixing our eyes on Jesus, the author and finisher of our faith.

After living more than four years with stage 4 ovarian cancer, Becky finished her earthly race early this morning. She didn't lose her fight to cancer. She never considered it a fight. While there were many difficult days during her cancer journey, she always considered it an opportunity and a blessing. She knew it was all a part of God's plan for her life and was determined to use it to give God glory and share the confidence she had in her heavenly future through Jesus her Savior. In that process, I know she inspired many by continually giving glory to God. We're thankful she had that opportunity and that she is now praising the Lord in heaven.

Thank you to everyone for the wonderful letters, cards, visits, prayers, and love you shared with us over these last few weeks, months and years. Becky appreciated all those who recently came to visit, sing, play music, and dance in our home and at the hospital. We are blessed to have had such a wonderful support system and incredible group of friends, including those who helped provide nursing support during the past weeks. While I know Becky touched the lives of many of you, please know that you have deeply touched ours as well.

While we are sad Becky is no longer with us here on earth, we rejoice that she no longer has any pain, discomfort or sadness. We rejoice that she is in heaven! There were many Bible verses that held special meaning for us during these four years, but this was her favorite: **1 Corinthians 15:55-57: Where, O death, is your victory? Where, O death, is your sting? The sting of death is sin, and the power of sin is the law. But thanks be to God! He gives us the victory through our Lord Jesus Christ.** What a blessing it is for everyone who believes in that victory. Becky knew that victory and believed it, and she has claimed her crown of life in heaven. **Revelation 2:10: Be faithful unto death, and I will give you the crown of life.**

For all those she has left behind, including her immediate family, her extended family, her friends and her Facebook family, the legacy she leaves is the strong faith she exhibited throughout her struggles with cancer. Her final prayer would be that each of us would continue to run the race we have marked out for us, keeping our eyes fixed on Jesus.

2 Timothy 4:6-8a: And the time has come for my departure. I have fought the good fight, I have finished the race and I have kept the faith; and now there awaits for me the crown of righteousness.

Chapter 13
Life After Death

I was incredibly blessed to be Becky's husband. Like the impact she had on so many others, she made me a better person as well – a better husband, a better father and a better grandfather. There were many beautiful responses to the final post. I wanted to include a few that reflected the Christian love she shared with so many and the faith she shared with others.

- "'Til he returns, or calls me home, here in the power of Christ I'll stand."

- What a wonderful meeting it must have been, Señora. We are all so grateful for the time we had with you.

- Such a beautiful example of how to live and die as a redeemed child of God. Feeling so blessed to have known this beautiful soul. Because of our Jesus, this is just, "See you later, Becky!"

- Today we mourn the loss of Señora Becky Lussky, yet we rejoice at her gain of eternal life.

- Señora, you were an amazing teacher, Christian role model, and dear friend. Thank you for the countless memories over the years. You were deeply loved and will be deeply missed.

- "And when your glory I shall see, And taste your kingdom's pleasure, Your blood my royal robe shall be, My joy beyond all measure; When I appear before your throne, Your righteousness shall be my crown, With these I need not hide me. And there, in garments richly wrought, As your own bride, I shall be brought To stand in joy beside you."

Hundreds of cards arrived after Becky's death. Most were from friends, but there were some from people I didn't know. We received private Facebook messages and emails from friends and friends of friends. One young lady who attended Becky's funeral service was there because of what Becky shared online. Immediately after the service, our family and relatives, along with some of our friends, went to the cemetery for the committal service. When we returned to the church an hour later, this young woman was still there, waiting to speak to me. This is my recollection of what she said:

> "You don't know me, but I've been following you and Becky on Facebook. I wanted to let you know how much she has meant to me during the past few years. She made a difference in my life and I wanted you to know that."

Becky would have been so thankful that someone had grown closer to the Savior because God allowed her to get cancer and write about it. Becky would have looked on this as one more blessing of cancer.

I received a nice note in the mail about five weeks after Becky died. It was from a friend we had not seen for many years. In the note, she stated:

> "Please know that many of us are still praying for you. That you and Becky allowed us to participate intimately in your lives through

Facebook as you dealt with her cancer means that many of us feel closely connected to you, almost like a part of your family. That was and is a blessing and a special gift to those of us who followed you and Becky through the difficult days. We can now give back to you with our prayers and our love."

What a blessing to have had so many praying for and supporting us during Becky's illness. What an additional blessing that those same people continued to pray for and support our family after she died. The connections we made with people through social media posts helped us during the journey and afterwards as well.

In spite of the fact that we believed God's will was being borne out in our lives through Becky's illness, there were times when I longed to go back to our lives before her diagnosis. Even though we shared some wonderful years while Becky had cancer, I wanted to go back and experience life together without cancer. I wanted Becky to live without pain and for us to make decisions without the cloud of cancer hanging over our heads.

I didn't know those feelings of longing for the past would increase after Becky died. Even though God brought me through the weeks and months after her death, I missed her company. I missed the comfortable companionship we had after decades of marriage. I missed being able to share things with her.

My sister, Marilyn, was diagnosed with stage 4 pancreatic cancer in May 2018. Though she was failing considerably by late December, she was bound and determined to come to Becky's funeral. It was special that she was able to be there at that time.

Marilyn passed away from her cancer just 47 days after Becky was taken home to heaven. At Marilyn's funeral, the pastor read some acknowledgments that Marilyn had written. She reflected on her thankfulness for the many people that were a part of her life. But what was most striking to me was her reflections on the period of time between when she was first diagnosed in May, 2018, and the time Becky stopped texting in late October of the same year. During that five-month period, Becky and Marilyn texted almost every day, mainly sharing Bible passages that gave them joy as they anticipated their journey to heaven. They built each other up in that future joy. In the written comments which were read at her own funeral, Marilyn noted how Becky showered her with meaningful words and always seemed to know the exact Bible verse she needed to hear. They were on the same journey, and shared a unique sisterhood of faith, family, and cancer.

Marilyn also noted that when she was first diagnosed, she had peace knowing this was God's plan for her life and she didn't have to be afraid. She said she didn't get emotional thinking about her cancer. She stated that the times she got emotional were when she felt all the acts of kindness that were shown to her through cards, flowers, gifts, acts of caring and prayers.

I held it together pretty well, dealing with Marilyn's death such a short time after losing Becky. But when the pastor read those specific words Marilyn had penned, the emotions were hard to contain. It was such a strong reminder of how many people had done the same things for Becky and me, and how it was those things that meant so much to us.

Throughout Marilyn's relatively short cancer journey, I had no idea she felt that way. Becky and I had both felt the same way. It was the incredible kindnesses people showed us. It was the Christian friends we had who supported us, prayed for us, and shared God's beautiful promises with us. It was especially during those times when emotions would rise to the surface. Until you are in that position, you don't know how much it means when your friends walk that difficult path with you and share in your sadness and grief. Marilyn's comments helped me understand we weren't the only ones who felt this way. Thank you, Marilyn, for that last lesson!

Becky's dear mother, Amanda, came down with a cough in late November, 2018. She thought she had pneumonia, so she wasn't able to visit Becky during the last two weeks of her life. When I spoke with Amanda on the phone during that time, she was concerned she wouldn't be able to shake the illness in time to come to Becky's funeral. When she went to the doctor, they took a scan and found there was some fluid buildup around her lung that was causing her to cough. The doctors drained the fluid just a few days before Becky died and did some tests on it.

The day after Becky died, Amanda learned she had stage 4 non-smoking lung cancer. That was totally out of the blue. Amanda tried one chemo infusion, but it was so difficult for her, she chose not to do any more. As another Christian woman of great faith, she was fine if this was God's plan for her to go to heaven as well.

Amanda departed this earthly life on March 20, 2019, three months and a few days after Becky died. At Amanda's funeral, a number of friends and family members mentioned to me what a joyous reunion we can imagine Becky and Amanda were having in heaven. While we don't know all the details of what heaven is like, we can rest assured there will be no sadness or pain. **Revelation 21:4: He will wipe every tear from their eyes. There will be no more death or mourning or crying or pain, for the old order of things has passed away.** We can picture that joy with the artist, Kerolos Safwat, in his painting entitled *First Day in Heaven*. We had this picture posted on a card next to Becky's hospice bed. It's not difficult to picture a similar joy that Becky, Marilyn and Amanda are now sharing in heaven.

I had lost my wife, my younger sister, and my mother-in-law within the span of three months. Each time I posted the information online, I felt a little self-conscious, as though some people might think I was looking for sympathy. In reality, while I appreciated the condolences, I really wanted to focus more on joy and happiness and less on sadness and grieving.

It could have been easy to get caught up in sadness and grief. I missed being able to share my experiences with Becky. I missed the unconditional love she had for me, even though she knew my weaknesses and failings. While it's a blessing to have children and grandchildren who love me, those relationships aren't the same as that of a loving spouse.

Throughout the days, weeks and months that followed, God gave me strength. When we gave our *Not My Plan* presentations, we focused on God's promises for us as we were living with cancer in our lives. Afterward, those same promises were just as powerful. I am still living, even as I feel the effects cancer has had on my life. I lost my wife, who was also my best friend and the most wonderful blessing God had put into my life. Yet His promises remain true. I can leave everything in God's hands according to His perfect will and His plan for my life. I miss Becky, but I can move forward, thankful she was such an important part of my life and trusting in God's plan for my future life as well.

I'm not going to write a final eulogy in this book. Becky was much loved by her family and friends and will be missed. There were three notes that were either posted or sent to us that I'd like to use as a final reflection of who she was and what she meant as she shared her Savior's love with others.

1. I'm not sure if Becky really knew what a profound difference she made in our lives. While my sister-in-law fought cancer for four years, Becky's posts about her own illness, lessons in faith, hymns, excursions and family celebrations all ministered to us. Through her openness and honesty, we were transported right beside you all. Her precious lessons about life and living fully were so real and so sincere. She absolutely poured herself out for others and taught us how to let God guide us to Him eternally. I have never had someone walk me through the valley of the shadow of death with such truth and such love. The Scriptures were her guide. Her posts are devotionals to me that I will always treasure. They will help me walk with Christ, pointed solidly toward Him.

2. To the woman that taught me my second favorite language and so much more, you will be missed. Mrs. Lussky was not only one of my favorite teachers, but she may have been one of the best human beings I have ever had the pleasure of knowing. Her strength, faith and dignity while going through some of the hardest times imaginable were an inspiration to me and so many others. While she will be so greatly missed here on earth, her legacy will live on in all of the lives she has touched. I say with absolute confidence that she will be rejoicing with the angels this Christmas, and I can think of no greater blessing for such a beautiful soul. Until we meet again, Gracias, Señora Lussky, ve con Dios.

3. Señora Becky Lussky, you will always be remembered as a beautiful, God-fearing and loving woman who helped so many of us as we struggled to find ourselves and our place in this world. You have helped so many of us understand the type of relationship that is possible with our Savior. You have been a beacon of hope and love. May you rest easy in His arms, free from pain and suffering. You leave behind so much more than memories.

Epilogue

I hope you enjoyed this book and found in it not only a reflection of some of the emotions and challenges of living with cancer, but also some of the joy, thankfulness, and encouragement we experienced during our cancer journey. We were blessed beyond measure, even through many difficult days.

Some of you may be familiar with a presentation entitled *The Last Lecture* by Professor Randy Pausch. If you have never seen it, look it up online and then watch it. All of it. It's entertaining, informative, poignant and instructive.

I really don't want to give away his punch line, but since I'm partially stealing mine from him, I want to give him all the credit for it. While I hope this book is an encouragement to *you* in your faith life, I especially wanted to write it for the grandchildren Becky and I share. I want our grandchildren to remember their grandmother as the wonderful, kind, and lovely person she was. Even more importantly, I want them to remember her as a woman of faith who wanted them to know their Savior as she did.

That's why this book is partially a memoir, partially a commentary on our journey dealing with cancer, and partially an encouragement to live in the shadow of God's grace, so that we all will enjoy the eternal blessings that come from knowing Jesus as our Savior. Throughout her life, *that* was most important to Becky. Heaven was her ultimate goal, and she wanted to take as many people there with her as she could.

In the end, we will all depart this earth. It's likely that everyone who has read this book has experienced or will experience the loss of one or more loved ones in their lives. Perhaps the most important message I can leave with you, and the main message of the book, is this: God's Word is powerful, His promises are comforting, and faith in Jesus as your Savior *does* matter when faced with suffering on this earth.

May God bless you and lead each of you to confidently lean on His grace as your comfort during the trials you face in this life, until you, too, are dancing with angels.

Made in USA - Kendallville, IN
1075066_9781952037016
04.09.2020 0729